National Interests in
International Society

A volume in the series

Cornell Studies in Political Economy

Edited by Peter J. Katzenstein

A full list of titles in the series appears at the end of the book.

National Interests in International Society

MARTHA FINNEMORE

CORNELL UNIVERSITY PRESS

Ithaca and London

First published 1996 by Cornell University Press
First printing, Cornell Paperbacks, 1996

Library of Congress Cataloging-in-Publication Data

Finnemore, Martha.
      National interests in international society / Martha Finnemore.
            p. cm. — (Cornell studies in political economy)
      Includes bibliographical references and index.
      ISBN 0-8014-3244-8 (cloth : alk. paper). — ISBN 0-8014-8323-9
      (pbk. : alk. paper)
            1. International relations—Political aspects. 2. Public
      interest. I. Series.
      JX1395.F485   1996
      327.1'01—dc20   96-13991

Printed in the United States of America

Cornell University Press strives to use environmentally responsible suppliers and materials to the fullest extent possible in the publishing of its books. Such materials include vegetable-based, low-VOC inks and acid-free papers that are recycled, totally chlorine-free, or partly composed of nonwood fibers. Books that bear the logo of the FSC (Forest Stewardship Council) use paper taken from forests that have been inspected and certified as meeting the highest standards for environmental and social responsibility. For further information, visit our website at www.cornellpress.cornell.edu.

Cloth printing   10   9   8   7   6   5   4   3   2   1
Paperback printing   10   9   8   7   6   5   4

For my family

Contents

Preface

The premise of this book is that much of international politics is about defining rather than defending national interests. Political science has focused its attention on the problem of how states pursue their interests. Pursuing interests, however, is only a part of what international politics is about. Before states can pursue their interests, they have to figure out what those interests are. This book asks questions about how states know what they want. That process of defining interests is as intensely political and consequential as our subsequent efforts to pursue those interests. I believe this is always true, but it is more obviously true at some periods of history than at others. During the Cold War, realists could make a plausible case that basic security interests at least were reasonably obvious and noncontroversial. Nuclear war was agreed to be a real threat, and avoiding it was the primary security challenge. The large literature on deterrence and arms races that came out of the Cold War and dominated security studies for decades could put aside questions about what our interests were. Our interests were to avoid annihilation, and they were not much contested.

The result of this world political situation both in universities and in the policy establishment was fascination with rational choice and strategic interaction as guides to policy. In a world where basic interests appeared clear and pursuit of them was imperative, these frameworks, which take interests as given, provided tools for analysis that seemed both appropriate and tractable. Thomas Schelling and those who followed strongly influenced both academics and policymakers in the ways they thought about U.S. foreign policy. In Washington, this perspective produced "rational" strategic policies of deterrence such as mutual assured destruction (MAD). In universities, these scholars provided recipes for training graduate students and templates for designing research that generated large rationalist literatures in both security and political economy on topics ranging from security to monetary coordination.

However, even the Cold War did not define interests in a whole range of issue areas. It may have set some basic guidelines for security policies and for economic and development policies (to oppose communism we needed to promote markets and democracy), but it did not narrow the set of possible goals very much, and it provided no guidance in areas such as environmental policy which had few Cold War connections. Even in the realm of security, basic interests were often not obvious and were fraught with controversy—as the Vietnam experience made clear.

After the Cold War, security interests or interests of any kind are even more difficult to discern. The organizing principle of U.S. foreign policy for more than a generation is gone. The basic premise of a generation of scholars—bipolarity—has collapsed and with it much of their power to explain and predict behavior. Here in Washington policymakers are scrambling for a policy. The lack of "vision" is not a problem peculiar to one administration or one party. It is a national problem. We no longer know our place in the world and much, I believe even most, of the politicking here concerns figuring out what U.S. interests are. It is time for international relations scholars, too, to attend to this problem.

The rational choice and strategic interaction literatures have succeeded in large part by ignoring a wide range of crucial political problems. They have made contributions by doing so but the value of those is dependent upon the assumptions on which they rest. One of those assumptions is unproblematic interests. Another is rational means-ends calculations as the dominant mode of human interaction. In this book I question both assumptions. Rationality, in this means-ends sense, is overrated in contemporary political scholarship, and often interests are not obvious. The goal of this book is to show how this is so and to offer alternative ways of thinking about politics that allow us to ask questions previously ignored.

The person who learns most from any book is its author. In writing this book, I have learned a great deal from colleagues and friends who read portions of the manuscript and have helped me to think through the issues it raises. I owe them a large debt for whatever may be of value in the book and for a great deal of personal learning besides.

Steve Krasner and John Meyer have been involved with the project since its inception. Their advice, coming from very different intellectual perspectives, has contributed to a much better product. Philippe Schmitter encouraged me early to think about global change from a comparative politics perspective, which proved invaluable in designing the case studies. David Dessler, Shibley Telhami, and Alex Wendt all read the entire manuscript and offered extensive comments, which much improved the final version. Early versions of chapters have profited from the suggestions of more people than I can remember. Among these, with apologies to those omitted, are Michael Barnett, Jim Caporaso, Charles Chatfield, Fred Cooper, Lynn Eden, David Lumsdaine, Jim Goldgeier, Judy Goldstein, Peter Katzenstein, Beth Kier, Forrest Maltzman, Marilyn McMorrow, Henry Nau, John Odell, Francisco Ramirez, Nina Tannenwald, Richard Webb, and Steve Weber.

When I was halfway through writing this book, Peter Katzenstein asked me to become involved in his Social Science Research Council/ MacArthur project on norms and national security. The conversations among that extraordinary group sharpened my theoretical arguments and showed me a range of possible applications of them that I had not previously imagined. Two other people deserve special thanks: Kurt Weyland, who helped me to thrash out the initial formulation of these problems over innumerable cups of coffee, and Joshua Mitchell, who pointed out the philosophical implications of the arguments I was making and encouraged me to pursue them.

Material support for the writing of the book came from the MacArthur Foundation, both from its grant to the Stanford Center for International Security and Arms Control and from its grant to the Social Science Research Council's Program on Peace and Security in a Changing World. The Facilitating Fund of George Washington University also provided summer money for research and writing. The Brookings Institution provided a congenial and productive place to finish this book during my SSRC/MacArthur fellowship. An earlier version of Chapter 2 appeared in *International Organization* 47 (Fall 1993): 565–97.

My debt to my family, particularly to my husband, David Furth, is beyond measure.

MARTHA FINNEMORE

Washington, D.C.

National Interests in
International Society

CHAPTER ONE

Defining State Interests

How do states know what they want? One might think that this would be a central question for international relations scholars. After all, our major paradigms are all framed in terms of power and interest. The sources of state interests should matter to us. In fact, they have not—or not very much. Aspirations to develop a generalizable theory of international politics modeled on theories in the natural sciences and economics have led most international relations scholars in the United States since the 1960s to assume rather than problematize state interests. Interests across the states system had to be treated as both stable and roughly identical if systemic-level theory of this kind was to proceed. Thus, neorealist and neoliberal scholars currently dominating the field make parsimonious assumptions about what all states want. States are assumed to want some combination of power, security, and wealth. With these few assumptions, these scholars seek to explain, as Kenneth Waltz put it, "a small number of big and important things."[1]

These are good assumptions. States *do* want power, security, and wealth. But I take these scholars' modesty seriously. A large number of "big and important things" remain to be explained in international politics. Among them are things that bear directly on the explanatory power of these assumptions. It is all fine and well to assume that states want power, security, and wealth, but what kind of power? Power for what ends? What kind of security? What does security mean? How do you en-

1. Kenneth Waltz, "Reflections on *Theory of International Politics*: A Response to My Critics," in Robert O. Keohane, ed., *Neorealism and its Critics* (New York: Columbia University Press, 1986), 329.

sure or obtain it? Similarly, what kind of wealth? Wealth for whom? How do you obtain it? Neorealists and neoliberals have no systemic answers for these questions. If external threats and power constraints are not determinative, such questions can be dealt with only on a case-by-case basis by country specialists or foreign policy analysts. International-level theory is helpless and mute.

This book addresses that silence. In it I develop a systemic approach to understanding state interests and state behavior by investigating an international structure, not of power, but of meaning and social value. We cannot understand what states want without understanding the international social structure of which they are a part. States are embedded in dense networks of transnational and international social relations that shape their perceptions of the world and their role in that world. States are *socialized* to want certain things by the international society in which they and the people in them live.

Ultimately, power and wealth are means, not ends. States must decide what to do with them. States may not always know what they want or how to use their resources. Foreign policy debates after the Cold War make this clear. Interests are not just "out there" waiting to be discovered; they are constructed through social interaction. States want to avoid invasion, extinction, and economic collapse, but for most states most of the time these negative interests do not narrow the set of possible wants very much. There remains a wide range of goals and values states could espouse in a wide variety of policy areas. Domestic politics can play a large, sometimes determining, role in defining national goals and interests, but as the cases here make clear, domestic politics and local conditions cannot explain many of the interests articulated and policy choices made.[2]

State interests are defined in the context of internationally held norms and understandings about what is good and appropriate. That normative context influences the behavior of decisionmakers and of mass publics who may choose and constrain those decisionmakers. The normative context also changes over time, and as internationally held norms and values change, they create coordinated shifts in state interests and behavior across the system. It is these patterns of coordinated, system-wide

2. Of course, as domestic politics become increasingly permeated by transnational influences, this may become another conduit whereby international norms and values are incorporated into state interests. Rosenau's turbulence work investigates such processes, as does much of the recent literature on transnational relations. James N. Rosenau, *Turbulence in World Politics* (Princeton: Princeton University Press, 1990). See also Thomas Risse-Kappen, ed., *Bringing Transnational Relations Back In: Non-State Actors, Domestic Structures, and International Institutions* (Cambridge: Cambridge University Press, 1995).

redefinition of interests that look odd from conventional perspectives and that this book addresses. The cases presented here demonstrate that states' redefinitions of interest are often not the result of external threats or demands by domestic groups. Rather, they are shaped by internationally shared norms and values that structure and give meaning to international political life.

Like much of social life, international social life is highly organized. Social relationships in international life may be informal, but many, especially those that most directly affect states, are structured and channeled through bureaucracies. Organization theorists have long recognized the role of norms in shaping organizational behavior inside and among bureaucracies. Some, especially those trained in economics, have emphasized the role of norms as tools of utility-maximizing firms in coordinating behavior and facilitating Pareto-optimal outcomes. It is this strain of organization theory that neorealist and neoliberal scholars have marshaled to elaborate their arguments.[3] There are, however, other ways of thinking about norms and their influence on organized social life. Sociologists studying organizations have emphasized their role in institutionalizing and propagating cultural norms—norms that define identities, interests, and social realities for the people who inhabit those organizations.

This book draws on these sociological insights to demonstrate the influence of norms on state behavior. The case studies examine the activity of three international organizations (IOs), two governmental and one nongovernmental, that are active in three different issue areas. Each case shows ways in which IOs socialize states to accept new political goals and new values that have lasting impacts on the conduct of war, the workings of the international political economy, and the structure of states themselves.

Where most recent theorizing in political science has turned to economics for insights, my approach draws on sociology and sociological organization theory, particularly the "institutionalist" strain of analysis in that field. Methodologically, it is most closely related to what is coming to be called "constructivism" in political science in that it focuses on the socially constructed nature of international politics. Rather than taking ac-

3. See, for example, Robert Keohane's applications in *After Hegemony* (Princeton: Princeton University Press, 1984) and the treatment of norms as facilitators of collaboration in Arthur Stein, "Coordination and Collaboration: Regimes in an Anarchic World," in Stephen D. Krasner, ed., *International Regimes* (Ithaca: Cornell University Press, 1983), 115–40.

tors and interests as given, constructivist approaches problematize them, treating them as the objects of analysis.[4] My three case studies demonstrate the utility of this sociological approach for understanding international politics across different substantive arenas.

My first case applies the approach to changes in states themselves. States are socially constructed entities. As recent debates over medieval politics and European integration make clear, there is nothing inevitable or immutable about the state-as-actor that our theories have traditionally taken for granted. States are continually evolving. They take on new tasks and create new bureaucracies to carry out those tasks. Since, in an important sense, states *are* what they do, these changes in state function at some level change the nature of the state itself. Chapter 2 examines one relatively recent instance of this, the creation of new science bureaucracies. Since this took place in virtually all states at roughly the same time, regardless of their science capabilities, the nature of the interest is not well explained by conventional approaches. I contend that states were taught that a science bureaucracy was a necessary component of "the modern state" by an international organization, the United Nations Educational, Scientific, and Cultural Organization (UNESCO).

A second case examines the conduct of war. We in political science tend to think of war as a Hobbesian state of nature, where anything goes because survival is at stake. In fact, war is a highly regulated social institution whose rules have changed over time. Chapter 3 investigates one of those rule changes—the adoption of the first Geneva Convention in 1864—and explores the reasons states found these rules to be "in their interest." I demonstrate that this "interest" was created and taught to decisionmakers in states by a transnational, nongovernmental group of individuals who came to be known as the International Committee of the Red Cross (ICRC).

The third case applies the approach to issues of international political economy and investigates how notions of development have changed. Development used to be a simple function of rising GNP or GNP per capita. In the late 1960s and early 1970s, however, notions of develop-

4. The term "constructivism" comes from Nicholas Onuf, *World of Our Making: Rules and Rule in Social Theory and International Relations* (Columbia: University of South Carolina Press, 1989). The seminal work on social construction is Peter L. Berger and Thomas Luckmann, *The Social Construction of Reality: A Treatise in the Sociology of Knowledge* (New York: Doubleday, 1966), although Berger and Luckmann's arguments follow clearly from longstanding claims by Weber and Durkheim about the reality of "social facts." For an elaboration of constructivism and its relationship to other approaches, see Alexander Wendt, *Social Theory of International Politics* (Cambridge: Cambridge University Press, forthcoming.)

ment expanded to incorporate distributional concerns. The alleviation of poverty and the meeting of basic human needs became an essential part of all development policy and planning for both donor states and developing states. Chapter 4 examines how this process occurred and asks, again, how states came to accept such a change as being "in their interest." I argue that the World Bank under the leadership of Robert McNamara was instrumental in redefining development.

The cases do not and, indeed, cannot "prove" that this approach is "right." Proof of this kind is impossible in social inquiry. They can, however, demonstrate its utility. They point to a pattern of consistent failure of conventional approaches in explaining certain phenomena and offer an alternative explanation consistent with the evidence. The conclusion to this book discusses the implications of this kind of analysis for the way we do research. The approach has weaknesses; it also has important strengths. It complements rather than replaces existing forms of analysis. It explains what are otherwise anomalies in international politics, and it also focuses our attention on some philosophic issues basic to our discipline, questions about the ends of political life and the nature of political community. Discussion of these issues has been the core of our discipline for more than two millennia. International politics has largely avoided engaging political philosophy for the better part of this century. It is time to reopen that discussion.

WHERE DO PREFERENCES COME FROM?

The claim of this book—that states are socialized to accept new norms, values, and perceptions of interest by international organizations—has important implications for the way we think about the international political world and the way we do research. It reverses traditional causal arrows. We have usually taken states as the starting point for analysis and examined the ways in which they create and interact with the various bits of furniture in the international system—international organizations, treaties, legal structures, multinational corporations, other states. This analysis looks at the way the international system, here in the form of IOs, changes and reconstitutes states. We are used to speaking a language of constraint. The international system is said to be important because it constrains states from taking actions they would otherwise take. The argument here is different. The international system can change what states *want.* It is constitutive and generative, creating new interests and values for actors. It changes state action, not by constraining states with a given set of preferences from acting, but by changing their preferences.

The claims made here about the importance of norms and values also shift attention from the largely material conceptions of international politics espoused by neorealists and neoliberals to a more social and ideational conception. Material facts acquire meaning only through human cognition and social interaction. My defensive measure is your security threat; my assault on free trade is your attempt to protect jobs at home. We have long understood that different social meanings assigned to the same set of facts can create different behaviors and even lead to conflict.[5] We have paid much less attention to ways in which shared understandings of the material world create similar behaviors, and we have not thought much about what the implications of such shared understandings and similar behavior might be. Material facts do not speak for themselves, and attempts to make them do so have limited utility.[6]

In this chapter I outline a social structural approach to international politics and describe how its utility vis-à-vis conventional approaches might be demonstrated empirically. The empirical demonstration derives from the different ways in which preferences are treated. Conventional theories treat preferences as inherent qualities of actors. Their proponents would expect different actors with different preferences to behave differently. Similar action by dissimilar actors in the absence of constraint is anomalous under these theories. Such behavior is to be expected, however, within a social structural framework. International norms of behavior and shared values may make similar behavioral claims on dissimilar actors.

The next section contrasts conventional treatments of preferences with those presented in this book and elaborates a basis for empirical investigation. The view of the international system offered here, however, also has important implications both for the macrotheoretic orientations

---

5. The most prominent example of concern with this problem is the "security dilemma" created by the material indistinguishability of most offensive and defensive military preparations. The most prominent work on perception in the field is Robert Jervis, *Perception and Misperception in International Politics* (Princeton: Princeton University Press, 1976).

6. There is no a priori reason to think that shared understandings are ethically "good" or will lead to peaceful behavior. Intersubjective agreement on the desirability of a scarce commodity will cause conflict. Shared understandings enable imperialists to exploit and ethnic cleansers to kill.

and for the microfoundational understandings of behavior that re-searchers hold. Specifically, the case studies I offer suggest that our dis-cipline, which has been dominated by agent-oriented approaches, might benefit from attention to the structure side of the agent-structure debate. These studies also call into question the discipline's fascination with means-ends rationality as the sole mode of action and suggest that other logics of action deserve attention. I examine both of these issues—macrotheory and microfoundations—in subsequent sections of the chapter and conclude with a brief discussion of research design issues and the theoretical significance of this project.

PREFERENCES IN EMPIRICAL RESEARCH

Preferences as Inherent in States

Most theoretical approaches in international relations share one or both of two assumptions in their treatment of preferences. First, they may assume that preferences are unproblematic; that is, that states and other actors know what they want and that those wants are readily dis-cernable to researchers. Second, they directly or indirectly locate the source of state preferences inside the state. Comparativists and many foreign policy analysts tend to make the second of these assumptions but not the first. They often allow policy preferences as problematic by specifying state decision-making about policy preferences as the de-pendent variable in their research design and then go on to provide de-tailed accounts of the internal demand-making and politicking by social groups and state officials that go into the formulation of those preferences.

However, these scholars make the second assumption—that prefer-ences come from inside the state—implicitly by choosing single coun-try research designs. At one level, this kind of design simply creates problems of emphasis. By focusing research on actions in a single state, they reduce the likelihood of detecting international systemic or inter-national societal influences. But the problem in single country re-search designs is more fundamental. Specifically, such research designs run afoul of Galton's problem: that findings based on the analysis of causal relationships within states (or other units of analysis) may be dis-torted by inter-state (or inter-unit) communication and diffusion. Sin-gle country designs, focused on unraveling causal relationships within a country, implicitly assume that individual countries constitute independent observations. To the extent that diffusion processes operate and that countries learn from the international environment, findings based only on the analysis of causal relationships within countries may be unreliable.[7]

Theoretical approaches used by international relations scholars outside the area of foreign policy analysis tend to make both of these assumptions about preferences and make them explicitly. They assume that preferences are unproblematic, well known to both states and researchers, and that they are inherent properties of states. Scholars working in rational choice and strategic interaction frameworks are clearest about this, but less formalized research projects are similarly structured.[8] They assume preferences can be readily deduced from objective conditions and material characteristics of a state. Changes in policy preferences or the appearance of new policy preferences are understood as responses to changes in these conditions and characteristics. To the extent that this response mechanism is elaborated and researchers open up the "black box" of policymaking, they look inside the state for changed preferences and tie the changes to demands by domestic actors. Some change in material conditions reconfigures the interests of actors inside the state so that they are prompted to demand a shift in state policy. In this way, the proximate source of state interests is located inside the state rather than outside. This basic logic applies even when the conditions in question are external to the state; for example, when they concern state security and the power relations among states. The shift in power distributions may lie outside the state, but the preference for security is inherent in the state, and the way that preference is translated into policies and behavior is either unproblematic and consistent across states or depends on politics and decisionmaking within the state independent of transnational influences.[9]

7. Comparativists are intermittently aware of this problem. For an excellent discussion in a research context similar to that of Chapter 2 see David Collier and Richard Messick, "Prerequisites versus Diffusion: Testing Alternative Explanations of Social Security Adoption," *American Political Science Review* 69 (1975): 1299–1315.

8. David A. Lake and Robert Powell, "Strategic Choice and International Relations," manuscript, May 12, 1995, University of California at San Diego.

9. Krasner's attempt to elaborate a statist approach to international politics is a direct response to these implications of systemic, specifically neorealist, theory. The neorealist ontology of states with given interests is useful to researchers only if there are, in fact, stable, internally coherent preferences within states across time. *Defending the National Interest* is an attempt to demonstrate the empirical validity of that assumption. Stephen D. Krasner, *Defending the National Interest* (Princeton: Princeton University Press, 1978). My Chapter 2 gives an extended discussion of this internal preference formation in an empirical setting.

The assumption that these preferences are unproblemantic and readily deducible from the objective characteristics and conditions of states is, at least in part, a consequence of the aspirations of scholars to construct a generalizable and deductively-derived theory of international politics on the model of economics or the natural sciences. Simply assuming or imputing preferences as essential characteristics of the actors is a necessary part of the foundation on which such theories must rest. Without specifying a priori and exogenously both actors and their preferences, these theories cannot explain and predict international interactions.

The two major international relations paradigms, neorealism and neoliberalism, both rest on foundations of this type. Both begin by specifying three things: the relevant actors, the capabilities of those actors, and their preferences. Both then go on to explain international interactions as the result of relevant actors using their capabilities to pursue pre-specified preferences.[10] Neorealism is by far the clearest and most self-conscious example. Waltz explicitly specifies states as relevant actors, measures capabilities in terms of power, and specifies preferences in terms of maximizing capabilities.[11] Neoliberalism in the form most recently articulated by Robert Keohane is structurally similar. The debate between these schools is primarily over the content of preferences assigned—for example, the degree to which states pursue economic versus military power or absolute gains versus relative gains, and the nature of the anarchy they inhabit. States-as-actors and state preferences are still assumed, not problematized.[12]

10. To the extent that Gilpin and Krasner's well-known summaries of theories in the field are correct, other less state-centric strains of liberalism as well as Marxism fit this form: the dynamic of these theories is one of pre-specified actors pursuing pre-specified preferences. In fact, however, Gilpin and Krasner's characterizations do significant violence to Marx's theories, and radical scholarship has moved in more structural directions since the mid-1970s, as evidenced by the work of Immanuel Wallerstein and Robert Cox. Liberalism, too, is a more complex set of notions than these summaries suggest, and some forms of liberalism may be complementary to the kinds of analysis outlined here, as discussed below. See Robert Gilpin, *U.S. Power and the Multinational Corporation: The Political Economy of Direct Foreign Investment* (New York: Basic Books, 1975), chap. 1; Krasner, *Defending the National Interest*, chap. 1.

11. Kenneth Waltz, *Theory of International Politics* (New York: Random House, 1979).

12. I am simplifying an extended debate here. For good summaries and insightful analyses, see David Baldwin, ed., *Neorealism and Neoliberalism: The Contemporary Debate* (New York: Columbia University Press, 1993), and Robert Powell, "Anarchy in International Relations Theory: the Neorealist-Neoliberal Debate," *International Organization* 48 (1994): 313–44. My concern in this book is with what Powell would call preferences over outcomes (rather than preferences over actions), which he agrees are not addressed by these theories. This debate comes closest to addressing some of the issues raised here when it deals with the nature of anarchy. As Milner discusses, one issue that separates neorealists from at

The assumptions that state preferences derive from internal sources and that preferences are somehow inherent in actors are important to both the single country researchers and to neorealists and neoliberals. For the comparativists and foreign policy analysts, state preferences must be the result of internal politicking in order to justify their focus on single country case studies. To the extent that the sources of state preferences lie outside the state and are not rooted in internal demands and internal conditions, their research designs are faulty and their research agenda is misdirected.

Neorealists and neoliberals maintain that preferences must be derivable from imputed functional needs dictated by state conditions if these theories are to explain and predict in a Lakatosian and cumulative manner. The notions that states can be supplied with new preferences externally and that those preferences may be unrelated to state conditions or functional need (as in the cases below) pose problems for these theorists. Some analysts might argue that one could accommodate externally-supplied preferences simply by taking new preferences, incorporating them into the state's utility function, and proceeding with analysis as usual. To do so, however, would be "ad hocery" of the first order. If preferences and actors cannot be specified exogenously before analysis begins, then all claims to explain and predict in a parsimonious fashion disappear into post hoc rationalization. These researchers would then be reduced to looking at outcomes and constructing the utility functions or specifying the preferences that produce them.

---

least some neoliberals is the degree and form of "governance" that obtains even under anarchy. Most neoliberals conceive of this governance in a way that is sociologically very thin, containing little social content. Governance is understood to mean institutions, usually formal organizations, that create "rules of the game." The notion that institutions might also reconfigure preferences and actors is not often explored by neoliberals, but works by Wayne Sandholtz on the European Union and Andrew Moravcsik on liberal theory suggest that by pushing this avenue of inquiry bridges could be built between some forms of neoliberalism and the kind of sociological approach outlined here. See Helen Milner, "The Assumption of Anarchy in International Relations Theory: A Critique," in Baldwin, *Neorealism and Neoliberalism,* 143–69; Wayne Sandholtz, "Membership Matters: The European Community and State Preferences," paper presented at the annual meeting of the American Political Science Association, Washington, D.C., September 1993; Andrew Moravcsik, "Liberalism and International Relations Theory," Center for International Affairs, Working Paper 92–6, Harvard University, revised April 1993. The possibility of building bridges between liberalism and constructivism has been noted earlier by Alexander Wendt in "Anarchy Is What States Make of It: The Social Construction of Power Politics," *International Organization* 46 (1992): 391–425. I expand on these connections and their limitations in the concluding chapter of this book.

Preferences Supplied Externally: Learning versus Teaching

Much of international relations theory rests on the assumption that states know what they want. Preferences are treated as inherent in states; they come from within the state as a result of material conditions and functional needs. The changes detailed in this study suggest, however, that preferences may not be inherent in states and may not be wedded to material conditions. Instead, state preferences are malleable. States may not always know what they want and are receptive to teaching about what are appropriate and useful actions to take. How would we think about such a process theoretically?

Adherents to an internal demand-driven view of state preference formation might argue that the "learning" of preferences documented here can be explained within the more conventional learning frameworks used in foreign policy analysis. The international system is, after all, an environment full of uncertainty, and states, like most actors, suffer from bounded rationality. Boundedly rational actors operating in environments of uncertainty frequently look for solutions to their problems in the solutions tried by other, apparently successful actors. Imitation, in a world of uncertainty, is often a perfectly rational strategy to adopt. Imitative learning processes of this type have been documented by a number of scholars. Hugh Heclo's study of the creation of social welfare bureaucracies in the United Kingdom and Sweden, for example, describes the way state officials wrestling with social welfare problems deliberately reviewed the policies and bureaucracies of other states, particularly Germany, in crafting solutions of their own.[13] John Ikenberry documents emulation of British and Japanese privatization policies by officials in other governments attempting to cope with fiscal crises in the late 1970s.[14]

These processes differ from the phenomena I document in this study. In the cases just cited, state officials change policies because they are under pressure to solve some already-identified problem. In Heclo's account, there are domestic groups making strong demands for the creation or modification of social welfare programs. In Ikenberry's account, officials are responding to pressing fiscal and budgetary crises.

13. Hugh Heclo, *Modern Social Politics in Britain and Sweden* (New Haven: Yale University Press, 1974).

14. G. John Ikenberry, "The International Spread of Privatization Policies: Inducements, Learning, and 'Policy Bandwagoning,' " in Ezra N. Suleiman and John Waterbury, eds., *The Political Economy of Public Sector Reform and Privatization* (Boulder, Colo.: Westview Press, 1990), 88–110.

The problem for state administrators is how to respond to these demands. The impetus for action comes from within the state, even if the solution does not.[15] By contrast, in the cases I investigate, state officials were not responding to any pressing demands or obvious crises. They were not looking for a solution to a problem. Both the "problem" and the solution were supplied to states by outside actors. Prior to the actions of UNESCO, most states, especially less developed countries (LDCs), had no notion that they needed or wanted a state science bureaucracy. Similarly, European heads of state were not particularly concerned about treatment of the war wounded until Henry Dunant and the International Committee of the Red Cross made it an issue. Global poverty alleviation, while long considered desirable in the abstract, was not considered a pressing responsibility of states, particularly of developed states, until the World Bank under Robert McNamara made it a necessary part of development.

The difference between the processes Heclo and Ikenberry describe and those investigated in this book can be characterized as the difference between teaching and learning. In the first case, states learn from one another (or, potentially, from non-state actors such as international organizations), but the impetus for the learning process lies inside the states. What is causal in this process lies at the state or sub-state level. There are no active teachers in this process. To the extent states are taught, they are self-taught. In the cases presented in this study, however, there *are* active teachers with well defined lesson plans for their pupils. Other actors are setting agendas, defining tasks, and shaping interests of states. In the science case, international organizations and the experts they used taught states that they wanted or needed a science bureaucracy. In the Red Cross case, the ICRC taught states to take responsibility for the welfare and protection of suffering soldiers, even enemy soldiers, in wartime. In the development case, the World Bank taught states a new image of "the developed state" and new strate-

15. Foreign policy analysts have also examined other types of learning, for example, the lessons states learn from past experiences and the causes and effects of certain types of policy actions ("the lessons of Munich") and what they learn about the nature of other states or leaders in the system. Arguments about causes and effects in these types of learning tend to be state-specific, however, rather than system-wide; they might aim to explain U.S. policy toward the Soviet Union at a given time, for example, but do not claim to explain coordinated system-wide changes in policy. For that reason, they are not obviously applicable to the issues under investigation here. For examples and discussion, see George W. Breslauer and Philip E. Tetlock, eds., *Learning in U.S. and Soviet Foreign Policy* (Boulder, Colo.: Westview Press, 1991) and Jack S. Levy, "Learning and Foreign Policy: Sweeping a Conceptual Minefield," *International Organization* 48 (1994): 279–312.

gies to achieve that status. What is causal in all three processes lies outside states. Both the definition of the "problem" and strategies for solving it came from international organizations and the individuals who created and ran them.[16]

Receptivity to the teaching of preferences implies a more social character for states than is generally acknowledged in international relations theory. It implies that the international environment is more than a "billiard table" constraining state action. It implies that states are embedded in a social structure and are "socialized" to a degree not allowed for by the more conventional, self-contained conceptions of the state. The role of "teacher" for international organizations similarly implies a more active and causal character than most theories currently allow. Most international relations theories are strongly state-centric. International organizations may mediate state interaction by providing rules of the game, supplying information, monitoring behavior, or creating transparency; ultimately, however, they are understood to be creations of states and servants of state interests. According them more autonomous and causal status, particularly as shapers of actors or interests, would violate the fundamental structure of neorealist and neoliberal theories.[17] It would embed states in a more diverse context of causal factors and push beyond "the limits of realism."[18] Pushing beyond the limits of these theories is precisely what this book intends.

16. Ikenberry also discusses the role of "external inducements" offered by the International Monetary Fund (IMF) and various development banks in states' decisions to adopt privatization policies. However, these IOs do not play the kind of teaching role in his analysis that they do in my cases. They do not create or define the problem states are trying to solve; they do not create normative definitions and new interests in an analogous way. Rather, in Ikenberry's analysis, interests are essentially given and IOs are additional players wielding their own set of carrots and sticks in the internal governmental politicking process that defines policy. Ikenberry, "International Spread of Privatization Policies."

17. According IOs more causal status also stands in contrast to the theoretical claims of more "statist" constructivists, such as Alexander Wendt, for whom the state is the unit of analysis. Privileging states may be tactically useful for such theorists in that it allows them to engage neorealists and neoliberals directly, but there is nothing about the logic of constructivism that would lead one to state-centrism. Indeed, the empirical findings in this book underscore the dangers of this assumption for constructivists. See Alexander Wendt, "Collective Identity Formation and the International State," *American Political Science Review* 88 (1994): 384–96, and *Social Theory of International Politics,* chap. 1. I take up this issue again in the discussion of constructivism and liberalism in Chapter 5.

18. Krasner lays out these issues clearly in his conclusion to *International Regimes.* The quoted phrase comes from his title. See Stephen D. Krasner, "Regimes and the Limits of Realism: Regimes as Autonomous Variables" in Krasner, *International Regimes,* 355–68.

STRUCTURE VERSUS AGENTS

The debate between theoretical frameworks in which states are treated as autonomous actors and those in which they are embedded in global structures is an old one and reflects the more general agent-structure debate that has been bubbling through social science for some years.[19] At issue here is essentially what is at issue there, and that is whether, analytically, one treats actors (i.e., agents), capabilities, and preferences as given and derives social structures from their interaction, or whether one takes the social structures as given and treats actors, their preferences and powers, as defined by the social system(s) in which they are embedded.

Political science has been dominated by actor- or agent-oriented approaches. Analysis generally proceeds by positing both preferences and powers for some group of actors, be they voters, members of Congress, firms, social classes, or nation-states. Macro-level political outcomes are then derived from the sum of micro-level behaviors by these actors pursuing their pre-specified preferences. In international relations, neorealism proceeds in this way. While Waltz in his *Theory of International Politics* argues for the constraining force of international structure on state actors, the structure itself is an epiphenomenon of the preferences and powers of the constituent states. It has no independent ontological status. More to the point, it is not generative. It does not create and constitute actors and interests. Instead it is constituted by them.

Structure-oriented approaches, by contrast, treat social structures as causal variables and derive actors and interests from them. Structures, not agents, are ontologically primitive and the starting point for analysis. The best-known arguments of this type in international politics focus on the structure of capitalism as causing a whole variety of economic, political, and social behavior. The world-systems work of Immanuel Wallerstein and the dependency literature both fit this rough form, as does the more recent work of such world-systems scholars as Christopher Chase-Dunn.[20] In all of these arguments, the structure of international capital-

19. For recent discussions of this problem in international relations see Wendt, "The Agent-Structure Problem in International Relations," *International Organization* 41 (1987): 335–70, and David Dessler, "What's at Stake in the Agent-Structure Debate?" *International Organization* 43 (1989): 441–73.

20. Immanuel Wallerstein, *The Modern World-System*, vol. 1 (New York: Academic Press, 1974); André Gunder Frank, *Capitalism and Underdevelopment in Latin America: Historical Studies of Chile and Brazil* (New York: Monthly Review Press, 1969); Fernando Henrique Cardoso and Enzo Faletto, *Dependency and Development in Latin America* (Berkeley: University of California Press, 1979); Christopher Chase-Dunn, *Global Formation: Structures of the World-*

ism creates actors (for example, firms and states) and gives them their preferences for expansion and gain.

There is no reason why the structure in a structural argument must be material and economic. Structures of shared knowledge and intersubjective understandings may also shape and motivate actors. Socially constructed rules, principles, norms of behavior, and shared beliefs may provide states, individuals, and other actors with understandings of what is important or valuable and what are effective and/or legitimate means of obtaining those valued goods. These social structures may supply states with both preferences and strategies for pursuing those preferences.

Arguments of this social-structural type are relatively new in American political science but have a longer history outside it. Surveying the field, at least three strains of research appear to fit this form: constructivism, the English school, and sociological institutionalism.

The best-known of these approaches in mainstream American political science has come to be called "constructivism." As the name suggests, scholars working in this vein share a general interest in social construction processes and their effects. They are concerned with the the impact of cultural practices, norms of behavior, and social values on political life and reject the notion that these can be derived from calculations of interests. They emphasize the importance of intersubjective understandings in structuring the ways in which actors understand what kinds of actions are valuable, appropriate, and necessary. These authors part ways with the more conventional actor-oriented approaches that Robert Keohane has called "rationalist" in that they elevate socially constructed variables—commonly held philosophic principles, identities, norms of behavior, or shared terms of discourse—to the status of basic causal variables that shape preferences, actors, and outcomes. In this way, they endogenize preferences. Preferences are strongly influenced and often constituted by social norms, culturally determined roles and rules, and historically contingent discourse.[21]

---

economy (Cambridge, Mass.: Blackwell, 1989). Wendt gives an extended discussion of Wallerstein's standing on the structure side of the structure-agent debate in his article, "The Agent-Structure Problem," 344–49.

21. Robert O. Keohane, "International Institutions: Two Approaches," *International Studies Quarterly* 32 (1988): 379–96. Keohane uses the term "reflective" for what I call constructivist. Since constructivism is the term preferred by those working within this framework, it is the term I use here. Prominent scholars who have been working in this vein for some time include Hayward Alker, Richard Ashley, Ernst Haas, Friedrich Kratochwil, and John Ruggie.

Constructivism is also the most amorphous and least defined of the perspectives emphasizing the causal nature of social structures. As the preceding discussion indicates, constructivists investigate a wide variety of social structural elements, and it is not clear how these different aspects of social structures relate to one another either conceptually or substantively. Conceptually, the relationships among principles, norms, institutions, identities, roles, and rules are not well defined so that one analyst's norm might be another's institution and a third scholar's identity. Substantively, similar problems exist. The social elements investigated by these scholars tend to be limited in scope, usually to one issue area. They focus on a particular social framework in which interaction takes place in discrete issue areas and show how these shared beliefs, norms, and discourse shape actors and preferences. These scholars thus investigate social structures in the plural with little attention to questions about the relations among specific social elements—whether they can exist independently or whether they must appear as a part of a mutually reinforcing collection of norms, institutions, and discourse. They do not explore the possibility of overarching social structures or of a single coherent structure that coordinates international interaction along coherent and predictable lines (as do some other scholars working within other social structural frameworks, described below).

Some of the earliest of these analyses appeared as part of the otherwise quite rationalist regimes literature.[22] John Ruggie, for example, elevates "legitimate social purpose" to the same level as hegemonic power in explaining the postwar economic order; he elevates social structures to causal status by arguing that recognition of the fact that liberal norms and values were "embedded" in U.S. hegemonic power is essential to understanding outcomes.[23] Similarly, Donald Puchala and Raymond Hopkins argue that recognizing the existence of normative superstructures is decisive for understanding colonialism and international interactions over food.[24] Ernst Haas has focused on cognitive processes more broadly and points to the shared experiences and commonly-held understand-

22. The issue-specific character of norms research in political science may in part be a legacy of the regimes scholarship from which it grew. Norms were (re)introduced into mainstream political science via regimes, which are explicitly treated as issue-specific in their definition: "principles, norms, rules, and decision-making procedures around which actor expectations converge in a given issue-area." Krasner, *International Regimes*, 1.

23. John G. Ruggie, "International Regimes, Transactions, and Change: Embedded Liberalism in the Post-war Economic Order," in Krasner, *International Regimes*, 195–232.

24. Donald J. Puchala and Raymond F. Hopkins, "International Regimes: Lessons from Inductive Analysis," in Krasner, *International Regimes*, 61–92.

ings developed within international institutions as determinants of outcomes.[25] Elsewhere, Friedrich Kratochwil has argued that the norm-laden character of language itself guarantees that systems of norms and social conventions will circumscribe any calculations of rational utility maximization in important ways.[26] More recent scholarship has continued the issue-specific and localized focus. Contributors to Peter Katzenstein's volume, *The Culture of National Security*, investigate the role of norms, identities, and social realities in weapons acquisition patterns, weapons taboos, humanitarian intervention, the dynamics of specific alliances, and military postures in specific countries.[27]

Each of these authors identifies a different socially constructed variable as causal and describes the causal process in a slightly different way, but all share a willingness to make social structures causal as well as a belief that these structures mold preferences in important ways. Liberal norms and principles shape U.S. preferences about how to exercise its power. Norms about self-determination and the avoidance of starvation shaped state preferences in the areas of colonialism and food. Preferences are the creation of larger social structures. They are endogenized in these approaches rather than treated exogenously.

A second approach to social structures as causal variables can be found in what has been called the English School, best known to American scholars through the work of Hedley Bull.[28] Despite debates in recent years over whether this collection of scholars can legitimately be called a "school,"[29] these authors certainly share methods and per-

25. Ernst Haas, *When Knowledge Is Power: Three Models of Change in International Organizations* (Berkeley: University of California Press, 1990); and "Words Can Hurt You; or, Who Said What to Whom about Regimes," in Krasner, *International Regimes*, 23–59.

26. Friedrich Kratochwil, *Rules, Norms, and Decisions: On the Conditions of Practical and Legal Reasoning in International Relations and Domestic Affairs* (Cambridge: Cambridge University Press, 1989).

27. Peter J. Katzenstein, ed., *The Culture of National Security: Norms and Identity in World Politics* (New York: Columbia University Press, 1996).

28. Other scholars working in this vein include Martin Wight, Charles Manning, Adam Watson, Gerrit Gong, Michael Donelan, F. S. Northedge, Robert Purnell, James Mayall, and John Vincent. Although Bull was not the founder of this school (Wight and Manning probably deserve that honor), his work is best known to Americans and most directly engages the debates outlined here. For that reason, I use him as exemplar. The term "English School" is somewhat misleading since two of the principal proponents are South African (Manning) and Australian (Bull). A more appropriate term might be "the LSE School" because the London School of Economics has been the institution at which most of these scholars came together.

29. Roy E. Jones, "The English School of International Relations: A Case for Closure," *Review of International Studies* 7 (1981): 1–13; Sheila Grader, "The English School of Inter-

spectives. Methodologically, they espouse holism explicitly and posit an "international society" of states which affects state behavior and state-ness at the center of their studies. The emphasis of English School scholars on the "structure" (as opposed to "agent") side of the debate could not be clearer.[30] They are also explicit in their rejection of the notion that international politics can or should be treated as a science in the manner that adherents to agent-oriented approaches might wish.[31]

While they vary in their claims about the "thickness" and content of international society, these scholars agree that at its core lie some principled rules, institutions, and values that govern both who is a member of the society and how those members behave. In Bull's work, this content stems from his philosophical examination of the moral implications of order. From the notion that order is a relational concept (in that things must be ordered to some particular end) Bull derives three common ends of all societies, including the international society: security against violence, ensuring that promises will be kept, ensuring that property will be secure.[32] Elsewhere, Bull, Adam Watson, Martin Wight, and Gerrit Gong make historical arguments that the content of international society comes from the liberal principles of Western European democracies and became internationalized with the expansion

national Relations: Evidence and Evaluation," *Review of International Studies* 14 (1988): 29–44; Peter Wilson, "The English School of International Relations: A Reply to Sheila Grader," *Review of International Studies* 15 (1989): 49–58.

30. Barry Buzan's suggestion that we marry traditional and historically-focused gemeinschaft conceptions of international society with more contractarian and constructed gesellschaft notions offers an interesting constructivist twist to English School thinking. While he and I differ in our understandings of Waltz's systemic theory and its relation to international society approaches, Buzan's recommendation, like the one offered here, is an effort to put agency back in social-structural approaches. Barry Buzan, "From International System to International Society: Structural Realism and Regime Theory Meet the English School," *International Organization* 47 (1993): 327–52.

31. See, for example, Martin Wight, "Why Is There No International Relations Theory?" in Herbert Butterfield and Martin Wight, eds., *Diplomatic Investigations: Essays in the Theory of International Relations* (Cambridge: Harvard University Press, 1966), 17–34; and Hedley Bull, "International Theory: The Case for a Classical Approach" in Klaus Knorr and James Rosenau, eds., *Contending Approaches to International Politics* (Princeton: Princeton University Press, 1969), 20–38. For a discussion of whether this rejection of science and the use of methodological holism are related to phenomenological strains of thought in the English School see Jones, "English School", 3.

32. See the following works by Hedley Bull: *The Anarchical Society* (New York: Columbia University Press, 1977); "The Grotian Conception of International Society" in Butterfield and Wight, eds., *Diplomatic Investigations*, 51–73; and "Society and Anarchy in International Relations" in *Diplomatic Investigations*, 35–50.

of the West.[33] These scholars acknowledge a debt to and kinship with Grotius and an interest in natural law, although none characterizes his own work as based on natural law.[34] Again, what interests these scholars is how social structure—the shared moral and philosophical environment in which states exist—shapes and tempers state preferences and actions.

A third approach to social structures as causal variables has been developed in sociology under the label "institutionalist" by John Meyer and his colleagues.[35] In the sociological institutionalists' view, social structure is constituted, not by an international society of states, but by an expanding and deepening world culture. The content of that culture is not unlike the Western values discussed by Bull, Watson, Wight, and Gong, but the institutionalists are much more explicit in their discussion of the logic underlying this cultural expansion. They argue that the modern international system is governed by a powerful set of worldwide cultural rules whose core is the Weberian (and Western) notion of rationality. These Western, rationalizing rules created the modern state, a political entity based on rational-legal authority rather than earlier traditional and charismatic forms of authority. In the current international system, these rules continue to shape states as system subunits, both by providing them with "rational" goals, such as the pursuit of "modernity"

33. Hedley Bull and Adam Watson, eds., *Expansion of International Society* (Oxford: Clarendon Press, 1984); Wight, "Why Is There No International Relations Theory?" in *Diplomatic Investigations*, 17–34; Gerrit Gong, *The Standard of 'Civilisation' in International Society* (Oxford: Clarendon Press, 1984).

34. Hedley Bull does use the term "Grotian" to describe an approach similar to his own. Bull, "The Grotian Concept of International Society." However, in his later work, *The Anarchical Society*, he explicitly states that he is *not* making a natural law argument, therefore his argument cannot be completely Grotian. Note that the way Bull and the English School use the term "Grotian" is rather different from the way the term has become incorporated into American political science. In Krasner's discussion of international regimes, "Grotian" is construed so broadly that it is used to describe a broad range of approaches including those described earlier as "constructivist." Since few of the scholars in this large and ill-defined group have any interest in natural law—which is, after all, the main focus of Grotius' work—I believe this appellation is misapplied. Bull, Wight, and their companions are, I believe, much more faithful to Grotius in their characterization of his work and their use of his name. See Krasner's introduction and conclusion to *International Regimes*, 1–21 and 355–68.

35. Other scholars working in the framework include Albert Bergesen, John Boli, Ron Jepperson, Francisco Ramirez, Yasemin Soysal, David Strang, and George Thomas. Seminal works in this vein include Albert Bergesen, ed., *Studies of the Modern World-System* (New York: Academic Press, 1980) and George M. Thomas, John W. Meyer, Francisco O. Ramirez, and John Boli, eds., *Institutional Structure: Constituting State, Society and the Individual* (Newbury Park, Calif.: Sage, 1987).

and "progress," and by defining the "rational" institutions by which those goals will be achieved, for example markets and bureaucracies.[36]

The structure of the institutionalists' argument is similar in some ways to that of Immanuel Wallerstein. Both arguments are holist, giving structure ontological primacy and deriving actors from it. Both are global, emphasizing the causal status of a "world-system" (Wallerstein) or "world-polity" (institutionalists). There are similarities in the content of the arguments as well. Like Wallerstein, the institutionalists understand the existing international system as an outgrowth of a historically unfolding dialectic which has its roots in medieval or early modern Europe. There is, however, a critical difference between the two arguments. The dynamic force in Wallerstein's argument is material and economic: capitalism and markets drive change. The dynamic force in the institutionalist argument is cultural and normative: rationalizing rules about progress and modernity *create* not only capitalism and markets, but also bureaucracies, expanding individual rights, egalitarian notions of justice, and other distinctive features of modern politics.[37] Institutionalist arguments are thus social in a way that world-systems arguments are not. They locate causal force in the intersubjective, in powerful shared ideas and beliefs about the world, rather than in objective material conditions alone.

The institutionalists' approach is the most comprehensive and explicit formulation of an argument in which social structure is causal. Unlike the constructivists in political science, they view social structure as coherent and all-encompassing, for all of the various little social structures identified by constructivists can be linked to an overarching system of Western, rational values. Unlike the English School, which takes states as the primary actors, understands international society to be a society of states, and is primarily concerned with social influences on state actions, the institutionalists focus on a much broader range of actors. World culture can and does influence all sorts of organizations and individuals as well as states.[38] The global social structure of Western, rational culture

36. For an extended discussion of sociology's institutionalism, see Martha Finnemore, "Norms, Culture, and World Politics: Insights from Sociology's Institutionalism," *International Organization*, 50 (spring 1996): 325–47.

37. Wallerstein, *The Modern World-System* and "The Rise and Future Demise of the World Capitalist System," *Comparative Studies in Society and History* 16 (1974): 387–415. For an extended discussion of the way in which these arguments are holistic, giving ontological primacy to structure rather than agents, see Wendt "The Agent-Structure Problem," 344–49.

38. For an extended argument about the role of non-governmental organizations as carriers and creators of world culture see John Boli and George M. Thomas, eds., *World Polity Formation since 1875: World Culture and International Non-Governmental Organizations* (Stanford: Stanford University Press, forthcoming).

has ontological primacy over any component actors, including states. World culture defines and empowers actors, including states, sub-state organizations, and even individuals.[39] International politics is understood, not as the result of interaction among actors, but as an outgrowth of the structure of worldwide Western culture.

The three approaches described above illustrate the variety of different ways international social structures can be conceived of and treated as causal. They are not presented as competing views. In fact, it is not at all clear that they *can* compete, for it is not clear that they are mutually exclusive. For example, the logic underlying the institutionalists' arguments subsumes the other two approaches and their findings within the institutionalist framework. In institutionalist terms, the society of states described by the English School and the norms and understandings identified by the constructivists in political science can be understood as manifestations of much larger and more comprehensive world cultural forces. From an institutionalist perspective, the other societal approaches are not so much wrong as incomplete; they do not go far enough in imparting causality to social structure. Similarly, Ruggie's embedded liberalism analysis is not incompatible with the understandings of international society put forward by Wight and Bull, but it is only a single example of a much more widespread phenomenon.[40]

My purpose is not to test these social-structural approaches against each other; rather, it is to demonstrate the utility of social structural approaches generally against more conventional, agent-oriented approaches. The demonstration is possible because expectations about state action are dif-

39. John Meyer provides a discussion of the ways in which Western world culture has defined the individual as a social unit and endowed it with rights and worth not previously recognized. John W. Meyer, "Self and Life Course: Institutionalization and its Effects" in Thomas, et al., *Institutional Structure*, 242–60. For Meyer's account of the construction of the state as *the* site of legitimate political authority, see his essay, "The World Polity and the Authority of the Nation State," reprinted in the same volume, 41–70.

40. It is not clear how constructivists in political science and English School scholars would react to the sociological institutionalists' claim to have subsumed their arguments. There has been little published discussion among these groups. Logically, however, they would have to dispute the institutionalists on one (or both) of two grounds. Either they would have to attack the claims for a relatively coherent and unitary culture spread across the world or they would have to attack claims about the Western, Weberian content of that culture. Since one could do research on both the content and coherence of global social structures, the debate would be an interesting one. I take up this issue again in Chapter 5. For a different and more detailed taxonomy of social-structural and other approaches see Wendt, *Social Theory of International Politics*, chap. 1, and Ron Jepperson, Alexander Wendt, and Peter J. Katzenstein, "Norms, Identity, Culture, and National Security," in Katzenstein, ed., *The Culture of National Security*.

ferent depending upon where the source of state preferences lie. As was noted earlier, each type of approach specifies a different source for state action and the preferences that drive that action. If preferences are inherent in or properties of states, formulated through internal demands by state and social actors, one would expect states with different characteristics and different functional needs to act differently. Similar actions in the face of different conditions or characteristics would be anomalous. However, from a social-structural perspective, such similar action would have an obvious cause. International norms, shared beliefs, discourse, culture, and other social structures may make uniform behavioral claims upon dissimilar actors. They may shape and define the preferences of actors in ways not related to internal conditions, characteristics, or functional need.

Patterns of change are one indicator that social structures are at work. Rapid global changes across dissimilar units suggest structure-level rather than agent-level causes. They do not, however, prove them. One also needs to specify the mechanism of change and show the common source of the new preference and behavior. For this reason each of the cases traces the process whereby the new preference was constructed inside an international organization and reveals the ways preferences were taught to states. These processes vary from case to case. The bureaucratic structure of the IO is critical in the World Bank and UNESCO cases but not in the Red Cross case (although it may be that the *lack* of a large structured bureaucracy was important in the ICRC case). Individual agency and moral principles matter a great deal in the Red Cross case, and to a lesser extent the World Bank case, but are not so important in the UNESCO case. While persuasion dominates the UNESCO and Red Cross cases, coercion is important in some aspects of the Bank case. IOs can thus affect state preferences in a variety of ways. What is important for this study is that they, and not states, are the agents of change.

NORMS AS SOCIAL STRUCTURE

Among the various elements of social structure, this study focuses on norms of behavior rather than discourse or culture more generally. I define norms in a simple and sociologically standard way as shared expectations about appropriate behavior held by a community of actors. Unlike ideas which may be held privately, norms are shared and social; they are not just subjective but *inter*subjective. Ideas may or may not have behavioral implications; norms by definition concern behavior. One could say that they are collectively held ideas about behavior.[41] This is not to say that norms are never violated—they are—but the very fact that one can talk about a violation indicates the existence of a norm. Many norms are so internalized and taken for granted that violations do not occur and the norm is hard to recognize. The norm of statehood as the only appropriate and legitimate political unit in international politics has only recently been placed on the table for examination by scholars; most scholarship has treated and continues to treat states as naturally occurring and inevitable rather than as socially constructed and historically contingent. Norms about the market organization in economic life have a similar taken-for-granted quality. Microeconomics has convinced us that somehow people in the state of nature would develop markets. It is only with the conscious attempt to engineer markets in former communist countries that we are beginning to realize just how much social and normative support is required for even moderately efficient markets.[42]

Evidence for the existence of norms can be found in at least two places. First, norms create patterns of behavior in accordance with their prescriptions. Each of the cases here documents such a pattern. Second, norms may be articulated in discourse (although this will not be true of

41. Recent scholarship on ideas in international relations, as exemplified by the essays in Goldstein and Keohane's volume, has been driven by many of the same concerns that drive my approach. See Judith Goldstein and Robert O. Keohane, eds., *Ideas and Foreign Policy: Beliefs, Institutions, and Political Change* (Ithaca: Cornell University Press, 1993). We all are looking to "occupy the middle ground," as John Hall puts it, between approaches that focus solely on material utility maximization and those that suggest cultural determinism. We differ somewhat in the ground we stake out, however. Goldstein, Keohane, and many (but not all) of their contributors hold fast to essentially agentic models and try to find room for ideas within those models. New world views are incorporated into actors' utility functions; ideas embedded in institutions become new "rules of the game" for strategic interaction. My argument is that this effort will not prove satisfactory in a great many important cases. Changing beliefs about what Goldstein and Keohane call cause-effect relationships may easily be incorporated into agentic paradigms; however, changing beliefs about what they call world views and, in some cases, ethical principles are not so easily incorporated since these involve fundamental shifts in the actor identities and interests that agentic paradigms take as given. Goldstein and Keohane are led down this road at least in part by their object of study—ideas defined as "beliefs held by individuals." This definition obscures the social nature and attendant consequences of a great many ideas, though some contributors to the volume, notably John Hall and John Ferejohn, deal explicitly with these issues. (See Hall's discussion of community on p. 49 and Ferejohn's discussion of intelligibility, pp. 228–29.)

42. For an insightful theoretical analysis of these issues, see Marc Granovetter, "Economic Action and Social Structure: The Problem of Embeddedness," *American Journal of Sociology* 91 (1985): 481–510. For an analysis of the social and normative supports needed for the initial establishment of markets in the West, see Joyce Oldham Appleby, *Economic Thought and Ideology in Seventeenth Century England* (Princeton: Princeton University Press, 1978).

the most internalized and taken-for-granted norms since they are often not the subject of conscious reflection). Because they are intersubjective and collectively held, norms are often the subject of discussion among actors. Actors may specifically articulate norms in justifying actions, or they may call upon norms to persuade others to act. To complement the behavioral findings of each case, I therefore examine discourse surrounding that behavior.

Structuring the analysis around discrete sets of norms in the cases is not intended as an espousal of any one of the three aforementioned conceptions of social structure. I do not believe that these arguments, as currently articulated, can compete and be tested against each other. A sociological institutionalist might read these cases and see them as part of a global expansion of world culture. The values embodied in the norms described—bureaucratic expansion of the state, increased concern with the individual, and expanding claims of human equality—are all compatible with the neo-Weberian world culture whose power is emphasized by these scholars. But the cases can also be read as discrete examples of social-structural influence with no necessary relationship to one another. In either reading, the cases challenge the conventional agent-centered paradigms.

CONSTRUCTIVISM AND THE RETURN OF AGENCY

Demonstrating the power of social structures—both *that* they influence states and *how* they influence states—is only half of my goal. The other aim of the project is to bring agency back into these social-structural accounts. For this reason, I investigate the origins of the normative structures influencing states: who created them and how they became embedded in the organizations that disseminated them. In doing so, I follow a constructivist research design. I emphasize the construction of social structures by agents as well as the way in which those structures, in turn, influence and reconstruct agents. Both agentic and structural approaches to social analysis are abstractions—simplifications that make complex phenomena tractable for social inquiry. As recent discussions of the agent-structure problem make clear, agents and structures are mutually constitutive.[43] To understand the relationship between the two, I

43. Wendt, "The Agent-Structure Problem," 350; Dessler, "What's at Stake in the Agent-Structure Debate?," 443.

first bracket agency and show the power of social structures in each of my cases. I begin with the structure side of the relationship only because that is the side most neglected by the dominant approaches in international relations. I then reverse the brackets and ask where the normative structures influencing states came from. In each case, I try to identify at least proximate agents of social structural change.[44]

What I am trying to explain in these cases is precisely what conventional approaches seek to explain: state behavior. I want to explain why all states create science bureaucracies at the same time, why they all agree to new rules of war, why they agree to redefinitions of development and changed policies accordingly. Explaining state behavior in a constructivist framework requires attention to the mutually constituted character of agents and structures. Consequently, each case study contains two strands of analysis. The structural strand, and the starting point for each study, examines coordinated system-wide shifts in state behavior and traces the cause of these shifts to normative claims pushed by an international organization. The agency strand examines how the international organization came to hold these normative views and the mechanisms by which it was able to "teach" those views to states. Thus, while the overall object of explanation is state behavior, this explanation must be built on contributing analyses of normative change within these organizations and the relationships between the IOs and states.

While my project and conventional approaches are similar in that they both try to explain state behavior, it is not the case that we have the same "dependent variable" because, of course, there is no variation in behavior (the "dependent variable") in my study. It is precisely the similarity in behavior where none should exist that makes these cases theoretically anomalous and worthy of investigation. A study of similarity rather than difference raises a number of basic methodological issues. Conventional wisdom in the discipline, reiterated most recently by King, Keohane, and Verba, is that such studies should be avoided because they cannot establish causal effects. This position ignores what such investigations *can* do. As David Collier has pointed out, studies of similarity can allow investigators "to *eliminate* some hypothesized causes, which can be a useful first step

44. Obviously, the loops of agent-structure relationships are complex and never ending. One can always ask about the social structures of nineteenth-century European bourgeois life that gave Dunant and his colleagues their humanitarian interests or about notions of social justice in Catholicism that gave McNamara his interest in poverty. Similarly, there could be material structures that influence these interests. My purpose is simply to show that both agents and structures matter and to provide some sense of how this is so.

in causal analysis." Elimination of hypotheses generated by conventional approaches is the first step in my case studies here. My second step is to generate an alternative explanation that is consistent with the evidence. As King, Keohane, and Verba are careful to point out, their methodological rules apply only to theory-testing, not to theory generation. My premise in this book is that method should serve theory, not the reverse. Theoretical anomalies should be investigated, and if those anomalies are anomalies of similarity, then we need methods to investigate similarity. King, Keohane, and Verba are correct about the limits of their methods for this kind of problem. That does not mean that we should ignore the problem; it means we should explore new methods and new approaches.[45]

To facilitate comparison across these cases, I have tried to make them as similar in theoretical structure and rhetorical presentation as possible. All cases seek to explain similar state behavior where conventional approaches would expect significant variation in behavior. All explicitly articulate alternative explanations for the state behavior under examination and look for evidence to support those alternatives. Finding none, all cases offer evidence concerning the role of IOs in bringing about the state behavior observed and investigate the reasons why the IOs acted to bring about these changes.

Analytically the cases are quite similar; however, the empirics of the cases do differ, and this necessitates some differences in presentation. Establishing the existence of a coordinated system-wide shift in state behavior is fairly straightforward in both the Red Cross and World Bank cases. The nearly universal adherence to the Geneva Conventions and global shifts in development goals have been widely noted and will be well known to most readers. The spread of science bureaucracies is less well-known, and I spend the early pages of that case study demonstrating that, in fact, there is an anomaly to be explained. I test alternative explanations in a variety of ways depending upon the nature of the data available. The science case lends itself to quantitative testing, and quantitative data are relevant to some aspects of the World Bank case. Such data are neither necessary nor particularly helpful in assessing hypotheses in the Red Cross case.

In testing alternative explanations, many of which I derive explicitly from conventional realist and liberal theories, the cases may give the im-

---

45. See Gary King, Robert O. Keohane, and Sidney Verba, *Designing Social Inquiry: Scientific Inference in Qualitative Research* (Princeton: Princeton University Press, 1994) especially 129–30; and the review symposium on this work, "The Qualitative-Quantitative Disputation," *American Political Science Review* 89 (1995): 454–81, especially the contribution by Collier and King, Keohane, and Verba's reply. Quotation from Collier is on p. 464.

pression that constructivism as a theoretical approach stands in opposition to realism and liberalism. This is not so: the relationship is complementary, not competing. My argument is not that norms matter but interests do not, nor is it that norms are more important than interests. My argument is that norms shape interests. Consequently, the two cannot logically be opposed.

To demonstrate this social construction of interests to neorealists and neoliberals, however, I need to show that it explains behavior that their treatment of interests, which tends to be both material and static, does not. For this reason, I have chosen cases that look anomalous from conventional perspectives. This is what gives the "competing hypotheses" flavor to the empirical studies and makes possible arbitration among the approaches on the basis of empirical evidence. In fact, though, my argument is not so much that neorealism and neoliberalism are wrong as that they are grossly incomplete. They can explain only a small amount of what goes on in the world, and attempts to apply these theories beyond that limited scope by imputing more and more interests less and less tied to anarchy will lead to results that are misleading or wrong.[46] The goals of this book are to analyze how this is so, to develop an alternative approach that can address these problems, and to demonstrate the use of that alternative approach empirically.

Constructivism is a social theory, not a theory of politics. It makes claims about the nature of social life and social change and suggests ways of doing research to uncover the links between structural and agentic forces. It does not, however, make any particular claims about the content of those social structures or the nature of the agents.[47] In this sense, it is akin to rational choice theory. Rational choice also makes claims about the nature of social interaction but not its content. Agents act rationally to maximize utilities, but the specification of actors and utilities lies outside the analysis; it must be provided a priori, before analysis can begin.[48]

46. Even close connection with anarchy may not solve these theorists' problems if they cannot agree on the nature of anarchy. See the debate in Baldwin, ed., *Neorealism and Neoliberalism*, especially chapters by Helen Milner, Robert Keohane, Joseph Grieco, and Robert Powell.

47. Wendt, *Social Theory of International Politics*, chap. 1. It is precisely the failure of Wendt and others to investigate the substantive content of social structures and marry constructivism with substantive theory that motivates my book.

48. Elster's recent work provides an interesting rationalist counterpoint to the arguments I make here. He has moved from a rational choice perspective to one in which social norms matter, but he continues to claim that this move can be made within a strictly agent-oriented perspective. No move to holism or structure analysis is required. He is correct only if one never wants to engage the questions I raise here—questions about the constitutive

Neither constructivism nor rational choice provides substantive explanations of international political behavior until coupled with some theoretical understanding of who or what are relevant agents and structures as well as some empirical understanding of what those agents might want and what the content of that social structure might be. Rational choice has been used in the service of agentic theories such as neorealism and neoliberalism in which agents are states and interests are some combination of military security and wealth. Substantive theorizing about social structures in international politics has received less attention, but both the English School and the sociological institutionalists point to the expansive power of the West and its notions of rationality as the core of an international social structure. This social structure privileges the state and the market—both rational (in the Weberian sense) forms of social organization—and emphasizes rules that support these institutions (such as protection of private property and organized monopolies on violence) as hallmarks of "civilized" conduct in world affairs. The international social structure has also privileged claims of human equality, increasingly so in recent years. All of these effects are documented in the case studies but these findings still leave unresolved many issues concerning the nature and content of international social structure. I take up these issues again in Chapter 5.

SOCIAL STRUCTURES AND LOGICS OF ACTION

Rational choice is called into service by theories that consider agents and interests unproblematic. When interests or actors become the subject of analysis, the dependent variable rather than an independent one, such methods become less useful. Rational choice requires knowledge of utilities; one must know what one wants before one can calculate means to those ends. Action without a clear understanding of what one wants must occur by some other process. The sociological institutionalists engage this issue and outline an alternative. Social structures—norms of behavior and social institutions—can provide states with direction and goals for action. The values they embody and the rules and roles they de-

---

effects of norms, about where norms come from and how they change. Elster treats norms as analogous to utility functions. They are taken as given and are regulative only, not generative, constitutive, or dynamic. Neither the origins nor the evolution of utilities and norms is accommodated by his approach. Jon Elster, *The Cement of Society: A Study of Social Order* (New York: Cambridge University Press, 1989) chap. 3, esp. 105–7.

fine channel behavior. Actors conform to them in part for "rational" reasons (for instance, because of the costs involved in "bucking the system" and the resources that become available through conformity) but also because they become socialized to accept these values, rules, and roles. They internalize the roles and rules as scripts to which they conform, not out of conscious choice, but because they understand these behaviors to be appropriate.

To say that action may follow a "logic of appropriateness" is not to say that it is irrational or stupid. Rules, norms, and routines may be followed for carefully considered reasons. They may embody subtle lessons culled from accumulated experience. Furthermore, determining which rules and norms apply in different situations involves sophisticated reasoning processes. It is, however, reasoning of a different type than that involved in consequentialist action, for it involves reasoning by analogy and metaphor rather than reasoning about ends and means. Actors may ask themselves, "What kind of situation is this?" and "What am I supposed to do now?" rather than, "How do I get what I want?" Thoughtful, intelligent political behavior, like other behavior, may be governed by notions of duty and obligation as much as by notions of self-interest and gain.[49]

The "logic of appropriateness" contrasts with a "logic of consequences" (such as that embodied in utility maximization) in ways important to the research here. The first is driven by social structure. Social structures of norms and rules govern the kinds of action that will be contemplated and taken. They also define responsibilities and duties, thus determining who will contemplate and take action. The logic of

---

49. Cognitive psychology has produced extensive research on the importance of cognitive scripts in individual behavior and the ways in which these override utility-maximizing choice. For general overviews of this material, see Susan Fiske and Shelley Taylor, *Social Cognition* (New York: Random House, 1984); R. E. Nisbett and L. Ross, *Human Inference: Strategies and Shortcomings of Social Judgement* (Englewood Cliffs, N.J.: Prentice Hall, 1980); Tom Gilovich, *How We Know What Isn't So: The Fallibility of Reason in Everyday Life* (New York: Free Press, 1991); Clyde Wilcox and Leonard Williams, "Taking Stock of Schema Theory," *Social Science Journal* 27 (1990): 373–93. March and Olsen, among others, have tied cognitive research into the organization literature and the study of political institutions. The terms "logic of appropriateness" and "logic of consequences" are theirs. See James G. March and Johan P. Olsen, *Rediscovering Institutions: The Organizational Basis of Politics* (New York: Free Press, 1989), especially chap. 2 for a more detailed exposition of the differences between these two types of action and an extended critique of the over-reliance on consequentialist logic in the social sciences. For an earlier formulation of this problem that makes perhaps stronger anti-consequentialist claims, see John W. Meyer and Brian Rowan, "Institutionalized Organizations: Formal Structure as Myth and Ceremony," *American Journal of Sociology* 84 (1977): 440–63.

consequences is driven by agents. Pre-specified actors or agents make means-ends calculations and devise strategies to maximize utilities. Norms, rules, and routines will be created as part of this process, but these will serve the interests of powerful actors; they will not survive long if they do not. The logic of appropriateness would predict similar behavior from dissimilar actors because rules and norms may make similar behavioral claims on dissimilar actors. The logic of consequences would predict dissimilar behavior from dissimilar actors because actors with different utility functions and capabilities will act differently. The distinction should not be overdrawn, however. Ultimately, like structures and agents, the two logics are intimately connected. Actors create structures which take on a life of their own and in turn shape subsequent action. Social structures create and empower actors who may act to overturn structures for reasons of their own. In any given situation both play some role. Separating the two, as I do here, is an analytic convenience not a statement about reality.

The case studies that follow illustrate both the working and interaction of these two logics. At one level, the science policy case demonstrates the power of appropriateness to prompt behavior even in the absence of any functional reason for it. States set up bureaucracies to coordinate science even when they had no science to coordinate. However, the genesis of this bureaucratic form was highly functional and consequentialist. Science bureaucracies appeared first in science-intensive states facing wars but later spread to science-less states. Thus, the construction of the social value placed on state involvement in science was driven by one logic; the spread of that value was driven by another.

This would imply that we can neatly associate consequentialism with the agent half of structure-agent analysis and appropriateness with the structure half: agents create social structures for consequentialist reasons but they spread for reasons of appropriateness. However, the other two cases suggest a more complex picture. There is no rational, functional, consequentialist reason for Henry Dunant to spend three days helping the war wounded, write a book about the experience, print it at his own expense, and spend months trying to persuade governments of the rightness, not the utility, of his cause. Such moral concerns about rightness and justice are more easily accommodated within some social-structural account that links Dunant's actions and those of the statesmen who signed the Geneva Conventions to Christian morality and Western civility. Dunant and the others claimed to act as they did because these actions were required of them as civilized Christian gentlemen.[50] In this case, the construction and dissemination of a new normative structure (the Geneva Conventions) both appear to have a large element of appropriateness mixed in. The World Bank case suggests yet another mix. The construction of poverty alleviation as an international responsibility served a straightforward utilitarian interest in bureaucratic aggrandizement because it meant huge expansion of the organization. But the evidence suggests that this was not, in fact, what prompted McNamara's actions. Moral concerns about right, just, and appropriate action played a large role in constructing the anti-poverty norm and persuading other states to adopt it. Again, both logics seem to have played a role in the construction and the dissemination process.

I have no grand theory as to why or under what conditions one type of logic might prevail or to what degree it will prevail. My concern is rather to point out that consequentialist utility maximization does not explain much of what goes on in international politics. Among other things, it does not explain global shifts in political goals of the kind investigated here. Coordinated and systemic reorientations such as these are better understood with social-structural accounts and constructivist approaches.

CASE SELECTION AND THEORETICAL SIGNIFICANCE

Any research design involves trade-offs, and this book is no exception. I present no cases that concern grand events of "high politics"; I present no cases of major wars or economic catastrophes. Critics might therefore argue that what I say here may be theoretically true, but empirically trivial. I have several responses. First, the task of challenging realists on their own "high politics" turf of national security has been taken up by myself and others elsewhere.[51] Second, and more to the point, making an empirical demonstration of the theoretical propositions is in itself

50. As was noted earlier, the globalization of Western standards of civilization and Western morality is a prominent topic among both English School researchers and sociological institutionalists. See Bull and Watson, eds., *The Expansion of International Society*; Gong, *The Standard of 'Civilisation'*; and John W. Meyer, John Boli, and George M. Thomas, "Ontology and Rationalization in the Western Cultural Account," in George M. Thomas, John W. Meyer, Francisco O. Ramirez, and John Boli, eds., *Institutional Structure: Constituting State, Society, and the Individual* (Newbury Park, Calif.: Sage, 1987), 12–37.

51. Katzenstein, ed., *The Culture of National Security*, contains chapters on such topics as weapons proliferation, weapons of mass destruction, military intervention, and alliance behavior, as well as analyses of the strategic policies of major states that show the importance of social variables in understanding behavior and outcomes.

non-trivial. Wendt, Dessler, Kratochwil, Ruggie, Onuf, and other early proponents of these sociological approaches have repeatedly been criticized for not demonstrating empirical applications.[52] This book does that. In making an initial demonstration, the terms of debate are always set by the dominant paradigms, so I chose cases for this study in which I could show that rational utility maximization was inadequate to explain the outcomes. The fact that two of the cases examine norms we might consider ethically "good" (humanitarian protection, poverty alleviation) is a comment on the paradigms I am engaging, not on my approach. Neorealists and neoliberals understand interest to be self-interest; other-regarding behavior is not well-explained and so creates the kinds of anomalies we look for when doing empirical research. But there is nothing inherently "good" about social norms. Social norms can prescribe ethically reprehensible behavior—slavery, violence, intolerance—as well as charity and kindness.

The case selection is also limited in that it focuses exclusively on IOs. Social norms and social structures have wide-ranging effects on all aspects of international life. However, in designing this study, I had to limit the range of social structural influences under investigation if I was to make any focused arguments about the causal properties of social structures. Again, the cases allow that: they were chosen to show one manifestation of social structural influence, that of IOs on states, and show it across a wide variety of issue areas. This creates some consistency across cases and allows for generalization.

Finally, I question the standards of empirical triviality implicit in the criticism. Yes, wars and economic collapse are undesirable. One reason to study international politics is to investigate ways to avoid them. But if things "matter" only in cases of war or economic collapse, and if such disasters occur because states pursue opposing interests, one would want very much to know where those interests come from. To answer the demand, "Show me that it matters," one must first understand in some general way how things come to "matter," how interests come to be constructed in such a way as to create violence and deprivation.

Much of the conflict of the twentieth century has been wars of national liberation, yet nationalism is a social and socially constructed interest. Post-Cold War military activity has been dominated by humanitarian intervention. Yet, as I have shown elsewhere, notions about who is human

52. See, for example, Goldstein and Keohane's comments in *Ideas and Foreign Policy*, 5–6, 26–27.

and deserving of protection and notions about legitimate intervention are socially constructed.[53] Much of twentieth-century political economy has been concerned with conflicts between growth and equity, but the equity goals (and arguably both goals) exist because of social understandings about what is appropriate and just in political life.[54] To understand war and economic change, one must understand the kinds of interests which lead states into conflict and the kinds of interests to which states direct their economic resources. Those interests are socially constructed. The construction process may be easier to discern in some cases than others. The cases that matter most according to any given set of criteria (most people killed, most change in state capacities, most movement of economic resources) may not be the cases in which the underlying processes at work are most visible. The cases here offer a theoretical window onto a process that may be obscured or varied in larger, more complex world events.

53. Martha Finnemore, "Constructing Norms of Humanitarian Intervention" in Katzenstein, ed., *The Culture of National Security*.

54. Arguably, both goals are socially constructed. The preoccupation of states with continually rising GNP per capita is distinctly modern. Prior to the sixteenth century and perhaps even prior to the nineteenth, economic success was defined by wealth in a much more static way.

CHAPTER TWO

Norms and State Structure: UNESCO and the Creation of State Science Bureaucracies

The structure of states is continually evolving. Since their establishment in Europe some five hundred years ago and, in particular, since World War I, states have grown both in terms of the variety of tasks they perform and in terms of the organizational apparatus with which they perform these tasks. International relations theory has had little to say about this process of state change, even though states are the unit of analysis in many, if not most, of these theories. Neorealists are explicit about having no theory of the state.[1] Neoliberal institutionalists who blackbox the state in order to engage realists are in a similar position.[2] Both schools would agree that international constraints might select out states with poorly adapted structures, but neither offers any explanation for ongoing structural dynamics among the remaining states. Other strains of liberalism suggest that state structure should respond to the changing desires of groups in domestic society, but these pluralist arguments have no necessary or obvious international component. They would suggest that state change should be idiosyncratic and dependent on the particular characteristics of each state. As a result, state change has been left to comparative and single country studies.[3]

1. Kenneth Waltz, *Theory of International Politics* (New York: Random House, 1979).

2. The form of neoliberalism articulated by Robert Keohane fits this category. See "Institutional Theory and the Realist Challenge after the Cold War," in David Baldwin, ed., *Neorealism and Neoliberalism: The Contemporary Debate* (New York: Columbia University Press, 1993), 269–300.

3. There is an internationalist thread in liberalism that begins with Kant's discussion of cosmopolitanism and has reappeared, albeit obliquely, in Andrew Moravcsik's recent formulation of liberal theory. Moravcsik initially summarizes the first core assumption of lib-

This chapter shows how states evolve in an international social context that shapes the direction of change in coordinated and consequential ways. People do not think about what states are supposed to be doing in a vacuum; they think about it in a world of other people thinking about what *their* states are supposed to be doing. States are reorganized, redirected, and expanded at least in part according to shared normative understandings about what "the state" as a political form is supposed to do. Some of those understandings are local, but many are shared cross-nationally and, very often, are developed and spread with the aid of IOs.

International organizations provide forums in which people from many states gather, often with the explicit agenda of rethinking what states should be doing. In this sense they are focal points for international community. They are places where people from many states gather to rethink the meaning of political community and the appropriate responsibilities of political organizations, usually states. This process is no more inherently consensual at the international level than it is at the domestic level. As this chapter shows, IOs are also places where people fight about what states should do. Furthermore, IOs are never neutral forums. Organization theory has long focused on perverse and unintended organizational behavior. Evidence from the case of science bureaucracies discussed here and from the World Bank case suggests that the filtering of norms through organizations may change them and their effects in ways not intended or anticipated by those originally doing the rethinking.

In the last 50 years, state bureaucracies designed to coordinate scientific research have sprung up in virtually all of the developed and in most of the developing countries. This chapter examines why states decided to expand in this way and why they made the change when they did. In political science and economics, most explanations for the appearance of these new pieces of state machinery describe this development as demand-driven. Some domestic group perceives a problem to which a science policy bureaucracy is the solution. Social groups, such as producers

eral theory as being "that states are embedded in domestic and international civil society" (p. 2), but the international component of society receives little attention of his subsequent presentation. Taking these claims about international society more seriously and developing their implications might lead liberals in directions parallel with the constructivist project outlined here. However, it would probably strain further the already fraying ties between neoliberal institutionalists and other liberals by making the former's nonproblematic treatment of states even more difficult to reconcile with liberalism's society-centered core. See Moravcsik, "Liberalism and International Relations Theory," Center for International Affairs, Harvard University, Working Paper no. 92–6, revised April 1993. I take up the issue of complementarities and contrasts between liberalism and constructivism again in Chapter 5.

of science (e.g., scientists) or consumers of science (e.g., technology-intensive businesses), may come to perceive that state coordination and direction of a growing science establishment is in their interest. State officials may come to perceive that the intimate relationship between science and security makes control of science in the national interest. Depending upon the perspective adopted, one would predict different configurations of science bureaucracies serving different interests, but in all cases the impetus for creating these organizations would be demand by state or societal actors that the government direct and control science.

I test these demand-driven hypotheses quantitatively by examining a variety of indicators of state conditions that have been argued to prompt demand and correlating them with the timing of the adoption of science policy bureaucracies. The results provide little support for any of the demand-driven hypotheses. Consequently, I examine an alternative explanation. Early in the diffusion of this bureaucratic innovation, two international organizations took up science policy as a cause and promoted it among member states. The chapter traces the process whereby one of these international organizations, the United Nations Educational, Scientific, and Cultural Organization (UNESCO), "taught" states the value and utility of science policy organizations.[4] The process was, indeed, teaching and not bribery: there were no significant material benefits to be reaped from setting up these bureaucracies as UNESCO directed. UNESCO did not fund the bureaucracies or provide material benefits as a reward for creating them. Rather, the creation of a teaching mission whereby UNESCO would supply the organizational innovation to states reflected a new norm elaborated within the international community about the relationship between science and the state. The norm held that the coordination and direction of science is a necessary task of the modern state and that a science policy bureaucracy with certain well-specified characteristics was the appropriate means to fulfill this task. Science was a national resource to be harnessed by the state so that the state could bring its fruits to citizens. This norm ran counter to earlier understandings of science-state relations, which held that science should be a transnational enterprise run by scientists—an international re-

4. The Organization for Economic Cooperation and Development (OECD) also promoted the creation of science policy bureaucracies among its members. The content of the normative dynamics among OECD states was slightly different, as those countries were less preoccupied with looking "modern." Nonetheless, the teaching activity and proactive role of the organization was very similar. See Martha Finnemore, "Science, the State, and International Society," Ph.D. diss., Stanford University, 1992, especially chap. 3.

source, not a national one. In this earlier view states were to treat science as they treated the arts: government sponsorship was desirable but government direction and control would stifle creativity.

In keeping with the constructivist mission of this book, the chapter examines the creation of the new norm and the way it displaced previous understandings. Unlike the other two cases, this normative change did not result directly from the conscious decisions of an individual or individuals to promote change. Intentionality is heavily filtered. The new science norm was constructed as a result of political changes made in UNESCO's organizational structure for reasons unrelated to science. The new science norm was a solution to UNESCO's organizational problems, not to functional problems in the science community or even in states.

I have chosen to investigate the creation of science policy bureaucracies as my specific instance of state expansion for two reasons. First, science is relevant to the formation of both economic and military policy preferences and so allows me to test the demand-driven arguments about state preferences broadly conceived. Modern warfare is a technology-intensive business, hence science should be relevant to states' policy preferences concerning security matters. At the same time, science and its technological manifestations are critical to economic competitiveness and so should be of concern to states in formulating economic or development policy.[5] Second, the coordination and direction of science is an area where states' internal conditions and functional needs are different. States presumably need to coordinate science only if they have some amount of science activity to coordinate or if actors in some other non-science sphere of activity (for example, the military or technology-intensive businesses) press demands for state intervention in science. As will be elaborated below, agentic or demand-driven arguments locate the cause of states' interest in science in some change in state conditions, specifically some change in military threat, economic development levels or the size of domestic science establishments. Since states vary widely in these dimensions, they presumably also vary in their domestic demands for coordination of science. Thus, science bureaucracies provide an instance in which agentic and social structural approaches would make different predictions. The former would expect the pattern of bureaucracy

5. Applicability to both military and economic policy preferences of states is particularly important as realists have begun increasingly to link "security" to economic prowess and competitiveness. For a well-known example, see Paul Kennedy, *The Rise and Fall of Great Powers: Economic Change and Military Conflict, 1500–2000* (New York: Vintage Books, 1989).

creation to vary with varying internal conditions and internal demand. The latter would expect creation to coincide with international normative changes.

BACKGROUND: THE DEVELOPMENT OF SCIENCE POLICY

The relationship between states and science by no means begins with the establishment of formal state science policy bureaucracies.[6] National academies and royal societies of science, many of which enjoyed some amount of state sponsorship and whose members were in frequent contact with government officials, date back to the seventeenth century. Similarly, state sponsored universities often housed scientists and their activities. However, state sponsorship of the sciences in this early period was understood to be analogous to state sponsorship of the arts; greatness and accomplishment in arts and sciences was a reflection of state power rather than a means to it. Further, patronage of this kind usually entailed minimal direction and control. Academies and universities may have benefitted from state funding, but they were not part of the state apparatus and were left free to pursue their work with a minimum of state interference.

The modern concept of science policy differs on both these issues. It understands science as a means to national power and consequently seeks to bring science activity under the control of the state. Most often this has entailed the creation of a new piece of state apparatus dedicated explicitly to the task. The first effort to do this was made by the British in

6. The history of relations between science and states is obviously much more complex than the summary overview presented here. For more on this subject, see Joseph Ben-David, "The Scientific Role: The Conditions of Its Establishment in Europe," *Minerva* 4 (1965), 15–54; A. Hunter Dupree, *Science in the Federal Government: A History of Policies and Activities to 1940* (Cambridge: Harvard University Press, 1957); Philip Gummett, *Scientists in Whitehall* (Manchester: Manchester University Press, 1980); Ros Herman, *The European Scientific Community* (Harlow: Longman Press, 1986); Eric Hutchinson, "Scientists as an Inferior Class: The Early Years of the DSIR," *Minerva* 8 (1970), 396–411; Daniel Kevles, *The Physicists: The History of a Scientific Community in Modern America* (New York: Alfred A. Knopf, 1978); Frank Pfetsch, "Scientific Organization and Science Policy in Imperial Germany, 1871–1914: The Founding of the Imperial Institute of Physics and Technology," *Minerva* 8 (1970), 557–80; Jarlath Royane, *Science in Government* (London: Edward Arnold, 1984); Ian Varcoe, "Scientists, Government and Organized Research in Great Britain, 1914–1916: The Early History of the DSIR," *Minerva* 8 (1970), 192–216; Robert Wuthnow, "The World Economy and the Institutionalization of Science in Seventeenth Century Europe," in Albert Bergesen, ed., *Studies of the Modern World-System* (New York: Academic Press, 1980), 57–76.

1915, when the government established the Department of Scientific and Industrial Research to wean British science and industry from continental, especially German, innovations, expertise, and technical equipment during the First World War.[7] A few Commonwealth members mimicked the British lead and established similar organizations, but it was not until after the Second World War that science policy bureaucracies became widespread. Before 1955, only 14 countries had such entities; by 1975, 89 did.

For purposes of this book, I define science policy bureaucracies as organs of the state which have as their primary mission the tasks of coordinating, organizing, and planning scientific and technological activities at a national level. I exclude from my definition the following types of organizations: (a) non-state organizations (such as scientists' professional societies); (b) organizations dealing with only one branch of science (such as the National Weather Service or medical and health organizations); (c) educational organizations whose primary mission is to train scientific and technical personnel rather than coordinate activities broadly; and (d) research organizations whose primary mission is to conduct research rather than make policy. This definition is based on UNESCO's definition used in compiling its world directories of national science policy-making bodies and so insures that the UNESCO activities chronicled below and my analysis concern the same phenomena.[8]

Demand-driven Explanations for Science Policy Organizations

Most explanations for the creation of new state bureaucracies trace the cause to some change in material conditions that reconfigures the interests of actors within the state. Functionalists might consider such an objective change to be sufficient as well as necessary for the new bureaucracy to appear. Others, less sanguine about the efficacy of political systems in meeting all needs and fulfilling all functions, would regard

7. Peter Alter, *The Reluctant Patron: Science and the State in Britain, 1850–1920* (Oxford: Berg, 1987), 201–13.

8. The first of these directories appeared in three volumes during the 1960s: *World Directory of National Science Policy-making Bodies*, vol. 1: *Europe and North America* (Paris: UNESCO, 1966); vol. 2: *Asia and Oceania* (1968); vol. 3: *Latin America* (1968). A second directory was published in 1984 as part of the *Science Policy Studies and Documents* series, vol. 59, entitled *World Directory of National Science Policy-making Bodies* (Paris: UNESCO, 1984). A second edition of the 1984 directory was published as volume 71 of the same series (Paris: UNESCO, 1990). I have made several refinements in the UNESCO definitions. These are explained in the appendix.

change in material conditions as a necessary condition only and look to the process by which demands are actually voiced and, once voiced, realized for sufficient conditions. But even in this latter set of explanations some material change must prompt the demand-making process. Thus, in most explanations there is some prerequisite condition associated with the creation of new state bureaucracies.[9] Three kinds of prerequisites have been considered relevant. The first are what I call *issue specific* conditions. Here, it is the situation in the issue area particularly relevant to the new organization that prompts its creation. Applied to science, this argument links the creation of a state science policy-making apparatus to the growth and strength of the domestic science community. An argument of just this type has been made by David Dickson to explain the origins of science policymaking in the United States.[10] In his view, the growth of the domestic science establishment prompted the creation of a state science policy apparatus in two ways: state actors saw a science policy bureaucracy as an opportunity to direct and control this new activity, and scientists saw such an organization as a potential conduit for state aid and benefits. Dickson's thesis would predict the adoption of science policy organizations to be highly correlated with domestic levels of science activity, for example, with the number of scientists in the country and the amount of R&D spending.

The next two types of conditions apply to the consumers rather than the producers of science. *Development* or *modernization* levels are argued to prompt the creation of science policy entities through the actions of the industrial consumers of science. The idea here is that as a state's economy develops it will become more technology-intensive and so require more scientific support. Economic actors therefore put pressure on the state to organize and supply this support, and a new science policy organization is the result. In many mixed economies these actors may be state economic actors: What is important for this analysis is that the purpose of demand-making is economic. According to this thesis, indicators of economic development, such as GNP per capita, should predict the creation of a science policy organization. *Security* conditions are argued to prompt the creation of science policy bureaucracies through the actions of military consumers of science. In the modern era of warfare, scientific

9. I have borrowed the term "prerequisite" from Collier and Messick's analysis of the spread of social security across states. David Collier and Richard Messick, "Prerequisites versus Diffusion: Testing Alternative Explanations of Social Security Adoption" *American Political Science Review* 69 (1975): 1299–1315.

10. David Dickson, *The New Politics of Science* (New York: Pantheon Books, 1984), 25–27.

prowess has been clearly linked to military success. Thus, states perceiving threats to their power or security will be pushed to find new and more effective technologies to meet those threats. The military in these states will demand that the state organize and support the scientific establishment for reasons of national defense.

The timing of science bureaucracy creation in Britain (during the First World War) and the United States (immediately following the Second World War) has led a number of scholars to draw causal connections between security concerns and science policy. Jean-Jacques Salomon, Harvey Sapolsky, and Sanford Lakoff all point to these wars, as well as another perceived security threat—the launching of Sputnik—as the catalysts for government interest in harnessing science to achieve national objectives in the United States and Europe. Having organized science to meet security threats during wartime with apparent success, these wartime institutions were then redeployed by states to meet peacetime objectives.[11]

Robert Gilpin makes a broader and more detailed security argument based on his investigations of French science.[12] He argues that France's creation of science policy organizations was the direct result of a perceived threat to French influence and independence from a preponderance of U.S. power immediately following World War II. At one level, this threat was understood militarily and led the French to use their science community to upgrade their defense establishment, notably to establish a separate nuclear strike force. But threats to influence and security in the French view were not limited to the military sphere. The French were also concerned about loss of economic dominance. American economic strength following World War II was viewed with trepidation, and American direct investment in France was viewed as a form of imperialism by a foreign power. The French spoke of a "technology gap" that they must bridge by harnessing French science in the service of French industry to protect French economic independence and integrity.[13]

Security understood in this sweeping way, as any threat to influence and independence, could operate in so many arenas that developing

11. Jean-Jacques Salomon, "Science Policy Studies and the Development of Science Policy," in Ina Spiegel-Rosing and Derek de Solla Price, eds., *Science, Technology and Society: A Cross-Disciplinary Perspective* (London: Sage, 1977) 43–70 and two other works in the same volume: Sanford Lakoff, "Scientists, Technologists, and Political Power," 355–92, and Harvey Sapolsky, "Science, Technology, and Military Policy," 443–72.

12. Robert Gilpin, *France in the Age of the Scientific State* (Princeton: Princeton University Press, 1968).

13. Ibid.

tidy objective indicators to test for its presence is probably impossible.[14] The narrower arguments about security threats understood in a military context are somewhat easier to test for. If armed conflict or the threat of armed conflict is critical, indicators of perceived military threat, such as defense spending as a percentage of GNP, should be correlated with the creation of science policy organizations. States perceiving military threats should be among the first to adopt science policy, and, conversely, relatively secure states should be clustered among the late adopters.

TESTING THE DEMAND-DRIVEN EXPLANATIONS

Each of these explanations posits a material condition that in turn sparks a demand for the state to adopt new tasks and to create new bureaucracies to carry out those tasks. While it would be impractical to investigate the demand-making process over a large number of countries, it is quite simple to check on the existence of conditions said to be prerequisite to those demands. The quantitative indicators of domestic conditions mentioned earlier have been compiled as described in the appendix for a sample of 44 countries, chosen to be globally representative in terms of both geography and development levels, and are analyzed below.

The testing of any global sample raises issues about comparability among states, particularly LDC and industrialized states. Cameroon and the United States, for example, are so different on so many measures that one must question whether the units of analysis are sufficiently alike to make comparison appropriate and meaningful. In this case, I believe the units *are* similar in ways that make this analysis appropriate to the research questions being asked here. The hypotheses being tested concern the behavior of states as a political and organizational form: they concern what prompts states to adopt new tasks and construct new apparatus to carry out those tasks. The hypotheses and the logic that underlies them do not carry caveats about degrees of state-ness, state capacity, or other potential limiting characteristics. Instead, they make arguments about the behavior of states *qua* states. Cameroon and the United States may be very different states, but they are both states, nonetheless. In fact,

14. For example, in the French case, threats to influence and independence extended to cultural matters and led France to pursue a number of foreign policy initiatives aimed at preserving and extending French language and culture in other states.

the chapter will suggest that what is going on in this case is a redefinition of the state as a political and organizational form, i.e., a redefinition of what is necessary and appropriate behavior for a state.

Figures 1–4 below show the distribution of values for each of the indicators of state conditions at the time science policy bureaucracies were created in these countries. A quick look at these figures reveals that none of the patterns supports a finding that any of these conditions is either necessary or sufficient for creation of a science policy bureaucracy. If any of these conditions were both necessary and sufficient, there would be a large cluster of adoptions on the histogram at that necessary and sufficient value. Instead, the adoptions appear to occur at a very wide range of values on all four of the variables. No single value of any variable appears likely as a necessary and sufficient condition for adoption. In fact, countries adopt these science bureaucracies at wildly different levels of all these domestic conditions. Some elaboration from the raw data make the extremely wide range of variation in values even clearer.

- Countries create these bureaucracies when they have as few as nine scientists employed in research and development (Congo) or as many as half a million (United States, Soviet Union).
- Research and development spending as a percentage of gross domestic product (GDP) can range from 0.01 percent at the time of adoption (Bangladesh) to 1.5 percent (France).
- Gross domestic product per capita in constant U.S. dollars can be anything from $118 per year (Pakistan) to more than $9,000 per year (Denmark) at the time these bureaucracies are created.
- Defense spending as a percentage of GNP can range from 0.7 percent (Sri Lanka, Mexico) to more than 10 percent at the time of adoption (France, Iraq, Jordan, USSR.)

The range of variation on the defense variable is more than a factor of 10; the range of variation on all of the other variables is a factor of 100 or more. Ranges of variation this large do not readily suggest any causal connection between sufficient state conditions and the adoption of science bureaucracies.

Similarly, the figures provide little support for the necessary condition hypothesis, i.e., that there is some minimum threshold value of these variables which triggers demand for the bureaucracy. If such a value existed, we should see very few (or no) adoptions at the low end of the value range of one or more of these variables; all values would

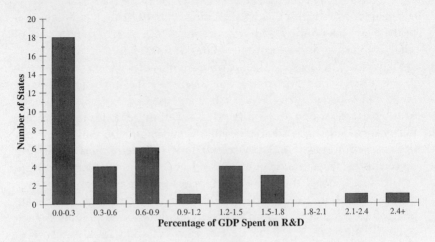

Figure 1. Research and development spending at time of science policy adoption

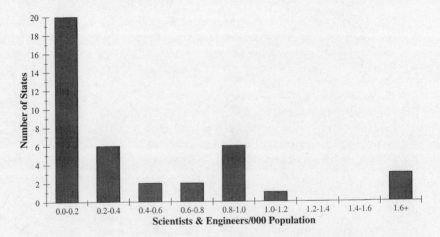

Figure 2. Scientists and engineers at time of science policy adoption

be spread across the upper end of the range, at or above the necessary condition level. Again, the far-flung distribution of values revealed in these figures and elaborated in the text above does not readily support this proposition. Rather than clustering at the upper end of these value ranges, there actually seems to be a concentration of values at the *low* end, particularly on the science variables. This is clearly not a bunching that would support the existence of a necessary and suffi-

44

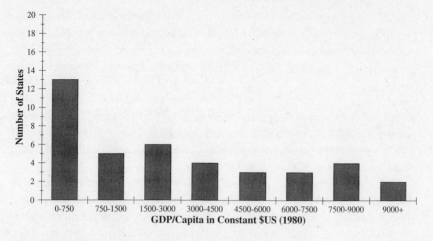

Figure 3. GDP per capita at time of science policy adoption

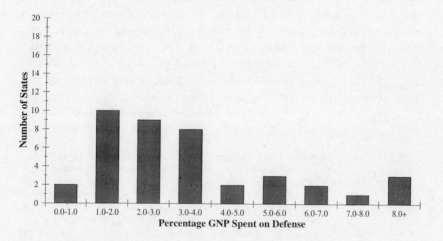

Figure 4. Defense spending as percentage of GNP at time of science policy adoption

cient condition, for the bunching in each case is accompanied by a large number of data points at the high end of each scale. Instead, it appears to be a strong negation of any necessary but not sufficient condition argument. If arriving at some minimum threshold level of these variables is supposed to trigger demand for a science policy bureaucracy, that threshold must be so low as to have very little explanatory power.

In fact, a large number of small, poor, technologically unsophisticated and militarily unthreatened countries created these bureaucracies in the 1950s and 1960s. It is this group that accounts for the clustering of data points at the low end of Figures 1–4. Guatemala, for example, created its Consejo Nacional de Investigaciones Científicas y Técnicas in 1966, when it reported having only 14 scientists employed in research and development jobs, spent only 0.01 percent of GDP on research, had a GDP per capita of $806 and, since it faced no serious military threats, spent only 1.07 percent of GNP on defense. The Congo and Cameroon were equally unlikely candidates for a science bureaucracy.[15]

At the same time, the histograms show that some countries create these bureaucracies at reasonably high levels of all the indicator variables. Significantly, the initial instances of this science bureaucracy creation fall in this group, thus suggesting that demand-driven explanations may fit some of the earliest adopters of science policy. Great Britain, the first adopter, clearly created its Department of Science and Industrial Research in 1915 for security reasons, to counter German advances in chemicals and machinery that were directly supporting the German war effort.[16] The establishment of the National Science Foundation in the United States in 1950 was explicitly related to concerns about military and industrial competitiveness and was strongly influenced by the creation of the atomic bomb.[17] French science policy-making, as chronicled by Gilpin, seems also to have been prompted by security and competitiveness concerns, albeit of a more general nature, as the French were

15. The Congo created its Conseil National de la Recherche Scientifique in 1963, when it reported having only nine scientists engaged in research and development jobs and when spending on R&D was only 0.11 percent of GDP. Gross domestic product per capita was only $253 that year and military spending accounted for only 2.04 percent of GNP. Cameroon created its Office National de la Recherche Scientifique et Technique in 1965, when it reported employing only 80 scientists in research jobs and spending only 0.16 percent of its gross domestic product on research. Gross domestic product per capita was $334 for that year; the country spent only 2.3 percent of GNP on defense.

16. Alter, *The Reluctant Patron*, 201–13; Roy McLeod and E. Kay Andrews, "The Origins of the D.S.I.R.: Reflections on Ideas and Men, 1915–1916," *Public Administration* 48 (1970): 23–48; and Varcoe, "Scientists, Government and Organized Research." Britain is not included in the quantitative analysis above because science data for that country in 1915 are unavailable.

17. J. Merton England, *A Patron for Pure Science: The National Science Foundation's Formative Years: 1945–57* (Washington, D.C.: The National Science Foundation, 1982); U.S. Congress, House of Representatives, Committee on Science and Technology, Task Force on Science Policy, *A History of Science Policy in the United States, 1940–1985*, Science Policy Study Background Report No. 1, 99th Congress, 2d session, 1986, serial R, 25–40; Daniel S. Greenberg, *The Politics of Pure Science* (New York: World, 1967), 68–148; Michael D. Reagan, *Science and the Federal Patron* (New York: Oxford University Press, 1969), 5–6.

concerned about a general loss of "influence" in the world, especially vis-à-vis the United States.[18]

But how do we explain the creation of science policy organizations in more than 100 other states, covering the extremes of science capacity, development levels, and military situations in the subsequent twenty years? Countries as dissimilar as Bulgaria, El Salvador, the Federal Republic of Germany, Indonesia, Italy, Lebanon, Mali, Pakistan, Sweden, and Czechoslovakia all created their first science policy bureaucracy during the peak adoption year of 1962.[19]

It will be argued that these two phenomena—the apparent responsiveness to state conditions in a few early-adopting states followed by a pattern of adoption unrelated to state conditions—can be reconciled in the following way: science policy bureaucracies appeared as an innovation in the international system in response to clear domestic demands in a few prominent developed countries; the innovation was then picked up and popularized by an international organization, UNESCO, for reasons of its own and spread by that organization to other states in which the conditions that might prompt such demands did not exist.

A SUPPLY-DRIVEN EXPLANATION

Since demand-side explanations for the creation of science policy organizations appear to be on weak ground for most states, I investigate an alternative: what if these bureaucratic innovations are not demanded inside the state but supplied from outside? In fact, most (roughly 70 percent) of these science policy organizations were created between 1955 and 1975.[20] Beginning in the early 1950s, two international organizations, UNESCO and the Organization for Economic Cooperation and Development (OECD), began actively promoting this science policy innovation among their member states.[21] In this section, I describe the promotion activities of one of these organizations, UNESCO, and present evidence that activities of that international organization were the impetus for widespread adoption of science policy. Such an explanation allows us to make sense of the data

18. Gilpin, *France in the Age of the Scientific State,* chap. 3.

19. "Peak adoption year" in this case means the single year in which the largest number of states created these science policy bureaucracies.

20. Extending the period by five years to include the years 1976–1980, the percentage of adopting states rises to 84.4.

21. For more on the science policy promotion activities of the OECD, see Finnemore, "Science, the State, and International Society," chap. 3.

presented earlier because it is consistent with both the low-end clustering on the histograms, indicating that many countries adopted these bureaucracies at very low levels of the indicator variables, and the timing of adoption across states, which is very rapid immediately after the international organizations begin to promote the science policy innovation. Specifically, I will argue that from its inception UNESCO has had to address two constituencies—the states who are its members and the professional experts in its substantive areas of concern. As will be described, the relationship between these two constituencies within the organization has changed over time, and these shifts were responsible for changes in UNESCO's programs, particularly the rise of science policy as an area of concern.[22]

As originally conceived, UNESCO was to be the United Nations Educational and Cultural Organization. Science was understood to be part of culture. The notion that science was qualitatively different from other aspects of culture and therefore merited special recognition in the organization's mission and title had to be fought for by scientists and science promoters in government during the preliminary meetings and negotiations that took place in 1942–1945. The fact that they succeeded in getting a piece of the new UN organization to serve their own interests was due in part to the organizational strength and coherence of the international science community and in part to their ability to influence world affairs, as recently demonstrated at Hiroshima.[23] The combination of these two factors convinced the president of the conference charged with establishing the new organization to propose addition of an "S" in the title with the following remarks: "In these days, when we are all wondering, perhaps apprehensively, what the scientists will do to us next, it is important that they should be linked closely with the humanities and should feel that they have a responsibility to mankind for the result of their labours."[24]

22. The following account of UNESCO activities is based on research done at the library and archives of UNESCO's Paris headquarters. While these contain a wide variety of documents authored by national governments, it must be acknowledged that carrying out the research at an international organization's headquarters does run the risk of bias in favor of an IO-driven explanation at the expense of a national one. A research design in which the science policy archives were consulted at a variety of national capitals in countries of different regions, development levels and facing different security situations would be superior. However, such a design was not feasible in this case.

23. Details on the lobbying efforts of scientists for special recognition in the embryonic UNESCO can be found in James Sewell, *UNESCO and World Politics* (Princeton: Princeton University Press, 1975).

24. Ellen Wilkinson, M.P., "Opening Address by the President of the Conference," *Conference for the Establishment of UNESCO, London, November 1–16, 1945* (Paris: UNESCO, 1946), 24.

Giving science a titular role in the new interstate organization was a way of recognizing the importance of science to the individual states but did not, in these early years, entail state control of science. UNESCO's early science programs were designed to serve science and scientists rather than states. They aimed to increase the sum of scientific knowledge and access to that knowledge without regard to national boundaries. The notion implicit in science policy, that science is a national resource to be developed by individual states, is very different from UNESCO's original notions of science as a transnational enterprise. Indeed, the principal rationale for internationalizing science and for bringing it under UN auspices in the first place was to free it from the meddling of self-interested and presumably self-aggrandizing states. Apart from the dangers of states exploiting scientific discoveries for military gain, state interference in science had long been understood to stifle scientific progress. Science was believed to proceed most efficiently and productively when left to scientists. Certainly this was the attitude of the League of Nations' Institute for International Intellectual Cooperation in the interwar period, and it continued to be the attitude of most scientists' professional organizations and individual scientists active in international affairs.[25]

Early statements of UNESCO's purpose with regard to science reflect this view. At the first session of the General Conference in November 1946, the Sub-Commission of the General Conference for Natural Sciences summed up the aims of UNESCO in the field of science as follows:

1. to establish a worldwide network of field science cooperation offices;
2. to support the scientific unions,[26] add to their number and assist them in their work;
3. to organize and operate an international clearinghouse for scientific information;
4. to support the work of the UN and its specialized services;

25. Early leaders such as Julian Huxley, the first executive director of UNESCO, and Joseph Needham, the first director of the Natural Sciences Department, wrote extensively on their views of science as a transnational activity. See, for example, Julian Huxley, *Unesco: Its Purpose and Its Philosophy* (Washington, D.C.: Public Affairs Press, 1947). Sir Henry Dale, who persuaded the establishing conference to accept science as a distinct part of the embryonic UNESCO and who had been part of the League's Institute for International Intellectual Cooperation, held similar views. See Sewell, *UNESCO and World Politics*, 78.

26. "Scientific unions" are scientists' professional organizations, such as the International Astronomical Union and the International Geodesy and Geophysical Union. Their umbrella organization is the International Council of Scientific Unions.

5. to inform the general public in all countries of the international implications of scientific discoveries;

6. to create new forms of international scientific cooperation (international
observatories and laboratories, etc.).[27]

Science policy and the promotion of member states' science capabilities
were not even mentioned.

Early UNESCO science programs conformed very much to these aims.[28]
Science cooperation "field offices" were set up in Nanking, Cairo, Rio de
Janeiro, and New Delhi to facilitate the movement of scientists and information around the globe.[29] Financial support was extended to nongovernmental organizations, particularly the International Council of Scientific
Unions, as a means of promoting cooperation among scientists, and more
of these unions were established.[30] Research institutes were established,
such as the Institute of the Hylean Amazon, the Institute of the Arid Zone,
and an International Computation Center, to bring scientists from different
countries together to work on problems of mutual interest. All of these activities provided services directly to scientists rather than states. The early organizational structure of UNESCO also reflected this understanding of
science and culture as transnational and often non-governmental. While
the General Conference was composed of equal member states, UNESCO's
Executive Board was to be composed of eighteen individuals, elected by
General Conference delegates for their distinction in the organization's
substantive fields. Board members were to serve on behalf of the Conference as a whole and not as representatives of their respective governments.[31]

27. Marcel Florkin, "Ten Years of Science at UNESCO" *Impact of Science on Society* 7
(1956), 123–24.

28. See, for example, "Activities of Unesco in the Natural Sciences during 1948,"
UNESCO archives, doc. NS/67.

29. The Rio office was moved to Montevideo in 1949, and in 1951 the Nanking office was
relocated to Djakarta in the wake of the Chinese revolution. In creating these field offices,
Needham (head of the Natural Sciences Department) was realizing the International Science
Cooperation Service he had proposed during the war. See Joseph Needham, "An International Science Co-operation Service" *Nature* 154 (1944): 657–59. For original plans for the
field offices, see "UNESCO Science Cooperation Offices," UNESCO archives, doc. NS/28/1947.
For a brief history of early field office program, see Florkin, "Ten Years of Science."

30. Specifically, UNESCO helped found the Union of International Engineering Associations and the Council of International Organizations of Medical Sciences. See Florkin,
"Ten Years of Science."

31. Note that this was a deliberate shift from the way in which the executive committees
of UNESCO's precursors, the Council of Allied Ministers of Education (CAME) and the
Preparatory Commission, were constituted. Both of these were composed of national representatives. See Sewell, *UNESCO and World Politics*, 34–36, 83–84.

The principle of nongovernmentalism enshrined in the composition of the Executive Board soon came under attack. Although board members were to be elected as individuals, the original UNESCO constitution provided that no state could supply more than one of its nationals to the board. In practice this put pressure on board members when their governments wanted to pursue particular policies through the organization. One high American official described the U.S. government bringing its board member back to Washington to "brief the hell out of [him] to try to get [him] to see things the State Department way."[32] Accounts of UNESCO Conference delegates from the period describe the decline of participation by scientists, scholars, educators, and writers and the increased presence of "government technicians" who viewed themselves as government spokesmen.[33]

In 1954, UNESCO members voted to amend the constitution and reorganize the Executive Board into a body of 22 governmental representatives. The shift toward a governmentalized secretariat was justified on several grounds. The reasons cited most often were financial: since states were footing the bill for UNESCO's operations, the organization should serve states. In the words of one official who left the organization about this time, the shift was "the price for financial support." A cynical French delegate, Roger Seydoux, predicted that with this change "the Finance Ministries . . . would become masters of UNESCO and its programme."[34] However, participants also understood the shift to be in keeping with a larger shift in the international climate from postwar Kantian transnationalism to Cold War Hobbesian nationalism. The original nongovernmental structure was a reflection of 1940s beliefs (or at least hopes) that ideas were a unifying force in the world and education, science, and culture could weave a web that would draw a divided world of nation states together. If, as Clement Atlee believed, "wars begin in the minds of men," then the UNESCO solution follows logically: "it is in the minds of men that the defences of peace must be constructed".[35] Harry Truman voiced similar beliefs in his appeal to the 1945 UN founding conference in San Francisco to "set up an effective agency for consistent and thorough interchange of thought and ideas, for there

32. Ibid., 169.
33. Ibid., 168–69.
34. Ibid., 169.
35. UNESCO Constitution, as reprinted in William Preston, Edward S. Herman, and Herbert I. Schiller, *Hope and Folly: The United States and UNESCO, 1945–1985* (Minneapolis: University of Minnesota Press, 1989), 315.

lies the road to a better and more tolerant understanding among nations and among peoples."[36]

By the mid 1950s this view had been eclipsed. At best, ideas were irrelevant to the intense power struggle raging in the world; at worst, they were viewed as divisive and dangerous things that states could not afford to leave to a collection of unaccountable individuals. As realpolitik replaced Kantian liberalism, states were reintegrated as major players in determining UNESCO policies to maintain the organization's credibility. Not surprisingly, the United States, then in the grips of anticommunist fervor, was the standard bearer for this new attitude. UNESCO came to be viewed as a political instrument in the Cold War; its purpose was to be a "Marshall Plan for ideas" which would block the expansion of "intolerant" communism. Failure to convert UNESCO wholeheartedly to its foreign policy agenda led U.S. officials to erect organizational barriers to contain and control the organization's influence. Chief among these was the International Organizations Employment Loyalty Board, established in early 1953 to oversee the employment of Americans in all UN agencies. Such screening ensured that American Executive Board members would be sympathetic to government views. This clearly flew in the face of nongovernmental principles.

While the Americans succeeded in replacing intellectuals of dubious leanings with patriots and loyalists, they failed in their ultimate goal of making the organization a tool of U.S. foreign policy. Just as their governmentalist reforms were enacted in 1954, the Soviet Union and several of its East bloc allies finally agreed to join UNESCO. Shortly thereafter came the influx of newly independent developing states with an agenda of their own, effectively blocking control by the United States or any other great power.

The shift from nongovernmentalism to governmentalism represented a shift in the balance of power among UNESCO's two constituencies. As the international climate changed and optimism about the utility of transnational activities declined, the champions of those activities—scientists, scholars, artists, educators—lost ground. Their rhetoric about building bridges to all mankind became less and less appealing to UNESCO's member states, who increasingly viewed the world as hostile and regarded the rest of humanity with suspicion. Thus, during the Cold War, states reasserted themselves as UNESCO's chief constituents, and UNESCO officials reshaped their programs to accommodate them.

36. Ibid., 33.

UNESCO's science activities soon reflected the shift in worldview and the organization's rediscovered constituency of states. While international scientific projects begun previously continued, UNESCO also became concerned with promoting science at the national level and began to focus its attention on helping states organize, direct, and expand their own domestic science establishments. Its preferred method of doing this was to help states to create a new state agency to take care of these tasks. As a first step in this direction, UNESCO conducted a survey of the national research councils of member states in 1953.[37] The stated purpose was twofold: to collect reference material for anyone asking advice on how to set up a research council and to provide background material for the establishment within UNESCO of an International Advisory Committee on Scientific Research, whose role would be to provide assistance to states seeking science policy advice.[38]

At this stage, UNESCO still viewed its role in science policy promotion as a relatively passive one; it waited for states to ask for advice and assistance. Following the 1954 reforms, however, the organization became more activist and science policy activities grew by leaps and bounds. In 1955, partly as an outgrowth of the 1953 survey, UNESCO convened a meeting of directors of national research centers in Milan. Thirty countries were represented.[39] The first agenda item for this meeting was discussion of "the role of national plans for the development of scientific research."[40] Papers presented at the conference by UNESCO staff members outlined the virtues of nationally directed science activity, discussed different models for such direction, and emphasized the role UNESCO would play in institutionalizing the planning of science policy.[41]

By the late 1950s, UNESCO had begun actively assisting countries in setting up science policy organizations. In 1957, when the Belgian government asked for help in setting up its National Science Policy Council, UNESCO sent the chief of its Science Policy Division to direct these activi-

37. Original survey analysis is contained in UNESCO archives, doc. NS/107. Survey results were also published as "Reports and Documents: Survey of National Research Councils for Pure and Applied Science in the Member States of UNESCO," *Impact of Science on Society* 4 (1953): 231–55.

38. Ibid., 231. See also Pierre Auger, "UNESCO and the Development of Research in the Field of Natural Sciences," *UNESCO Chronicle* 1 (1955), 5.

39. Final report found in UNESCO archives, doc. NS/124. See also Auger, "UNESCO and the Development of Research," 5.

40. *UNESCO Chronicle* 1 (1955), 26.

41. Several of these papers were later published in *Impact of Science on Society*. Most relevant is Werner Moller's "National Research Councils and Science Policy," *Impact of Science on Society* 6 (1955): 155–68. Moller was a member of the Natural Sciences Department.

ties.[42] UNESCO also provided assistance to the Lebanese government in creating a National Council for Scientific Research.[43] These activities of the Natural Sciences Department received a boost in 1960 when UNESCO's Pierre Auger,[44] then acting as a special consultant to the UN, issued a report entitled "Current Trends in Scientific Research." His first recommendation was that national scientific policy should be one of the "foremost preoccupations of governments. . . . States should make it their business to ensure [that the] interaction between the encouragement of scientific research, on the one hand, and economic and social progress, on the other, operates smoothly to the advantage of both. It is, at the same time, the duty of organizations in the United Nations family to assist States in this matter."[45]

Auger's detailed report, requested and approved by the larger UN, validated the science policy activities UNESCO had engaged in over the previous five years and provided a basis for formalizing what had been an ad hoc collection of activities.[46] Beginning in 1960, UNESCO General Conference resolutions included instructions that the director-general "collect, analyse and disseminate information concerning the organization of scientific research in Member States and the policies of Member States in this respect."[47] By 1963, the General Conference resolutions were more explicit. The director-general was authorized to assist member states "in the establishment or improvement of science policy planning and research organization, through sending advisory missions, conducting scientific and technological potential surveys, with particular regard to human resources and budgets, or organizing training seminars and, to this end, to participate in their activities in

42. The Belgian National Science Policy Council was established in 1959. "Survey of UNESCO's Activities and Achievements with Regard to Science Policy," UNESCO archives, doc. NS/ROU/100.

43. UNESCO archives, docs. NS/ROU/LEB, 1–23; also NS/ROU/100.

44. Auger had been the second head of the Natural Sciences Department after Joseph Needham and had recently retired from the secretariat.

45. Pierre Auger, *Current Trends in Scientific Research* (Paris: UNESCO, 1961), 220.

46. This report is routinely cited as the original basis for UNESCO's science policy activities. See, for example, Y. de Hemptinne, "UNESCO's Role in the Organization of Scientific Research," *UNESCO Chronicle* 9 (1963): 245. Also, see the opening speech by Alexei Matveyev, assistant director-general for science, to the Meeting of the Coordinators of Science Policy Studies in Karlovy-Vary, Czechoslovakia, June 1966, reprinted in *Principles and Problems of National Science Policies*, part of the Science Policy Studies and Documents series, vol. 5 (Paris: UNESCO, 1967), 12. See also UNESCO archives, doc. NS/ROU/100, 3.

47. UNESCO, General Conference, 11th session, 1960. *Resolutions* 2.1131, (Paris: UNESCO, 1960).

54

the field."[48] From this point on, the goal of spreading and improving science policy organizations was firmly entrenched in UNESCO's official science program.

What is interesting about UNESCO's program in regard to the questions raised in this chapter is that the language used is prescriptive but not evaluative and in this sense is normative. UNESCO officials simply declared science policymaking to be necessary and good without seriously attempting to prove that this is in fact so. "States *should* make it their business" to coordinate and direct science.[49] Or, as it was later expressed, "The development of science policy should be the responsibility of an organization at the highest level of government in the country,"[50] and "the Science Policy Programme of UNESCO is formulated on the basis of *the principle* that the planning of science policy is indispensable" for the coordination and promotion of scientific research.[51] These assertions are not coupled with any evidence that such bureaucratic entities actually enhance science capabilities. This omission is surprising given that, until only a few years earlier, conventional wisdom had held exactly the opposite—that government involvement stifled scientific creativity.

In addition, the language is universal; it promotes these bureaucracies as good for all states, at all levels of scientific capability. This ignores an obvious potential strategy for many countries, particularly LDCs—free-riding. Science, with its imperative to disseminate results widely and immediately, has many properties of a collective good. The economic advantages of being a copycat rather than a leader in technological innovation have been widely discussed in other contexts.

Thus, from a functional standpoint, it is not obvious why all states suddenly "needed" a science policy bureaucracy at that particular point in time. In fact, it appears that these events were not related to functional need in any strict sense. Rather, they constitute a redefinition of the norms and expectations of state roles with regard to science. Initially, scientists sought to harness state resources to further their own projects by claiming a piece of an interstate organization. To do so, they had to proclaim science an appropriate concern of governments. The debate over the "S" in UNESCO and Ellen Wilkinson's comments in proposing it reveal

---

48. UNESCO, General Conference, 13th Session, 1964. *Resolutions*, 2.112(d), (Paris: UNESCO, 1964), 32.

49. Auger, *Current Trends*, 220, quoted above (emphasis mine).

50. UNESCO, *Principles and Problems*, vol. 5, 87.

51. "The Proposed Science Policy Program of Unesco for 1967–1968," UNESCO archives, doc. NS/ROU/117, 1 (emphasis mine).

the scientists' success in this. However, when scientists, along with educators, artists, and other professionals, lost control of UNESCO to the member states, the situation did not simply revert to the status quo ante. The norm that science was now an appropriate concern of states remained firmly entrenched, but the relationship between science and states was redefined to reflect the new world climate and UNESCO's new dominant constituency. Rather than states collectively, within an international organization promoting and directing science as a transnational enterprise, Natural Sciences Department officials in UNESCO now argued that states *individually* should take responsibility for promoting and directing science within their own borders. By proclaiming science policy-making to be an appropriate and necessary function of states qua states and by offering themselves as a source of knowledge about this new function, UNESCO science officials successfully redefined their role in a way that was neither "irrelevant" nor "dangerous" to their new clients.

States' interest in and the success of UNESCO's efforts are related to the fact that during this period large numbers of new states were being created, virtually all of which were LDCs. While it was developed countries such as the United States and the United Kingdom that initially pushed for the reorganization of UNESCO's Executive Board to favor states for Cold War reasons in the 1950s, UNESCO's reorientation toward states fit well with the climate of national self-determination in the 1960s. Among the large and growing membership of newly-independent LDCs, the notion that states should and could promote and direct science, with all its economic and military applications, was popular. At the 1963 UN Conference on Science and Technology for the Benefit of Less Developed Areas, the agenda item Organization and Planning of Scientific and Technological Policies "yielded one of the most fruitful discussions in the whole conference, according to the official summary of the conference."[52] In addition to lauding science policy as an activity, conference delegates stressed the importance of building up in the developing countries indigenous programs of research. They argued that "just as no country could develop economically on imported goods, so none could develop intellectually on imported ideas alone."[53] For these states, science as a transnational activity spelled continued dependence. Science had to be a national pursuit to be normatively compatible with the na-

52. United Nations, Economic and Social Council, 36th session, "Report to the Secretary-General on the Results of the United Nations Conference on Science and Technology for the Benefit of Less Developed Areas" (E/3772), annexes, agenda item 15.
53. Ibid., sec. 181, 24.

tionalism of the newly created national state and to provide the state with means of resisting encroachments from outside.[54]

This national or statist conception is distinct from the original understanding of science that prevailed in UNESCO's early years. States were now understood to be the primary purveyors of development and progress; thus it was states, not scientists, that could best bring the fruits of science and technology to their citizens. Scientific knowledge could be translated into increased wealth, security, or improved standards of living only if it was harnessed by states and integrated into their larger economic and military establishments. Scientific capacity or "scientific potential" was viewed as a national resource, not as a portion of some larger collectively held international resource.

The redefinition of science as a state concern did not necessarily have negative implications for the independence or productivity of the scientific community. In fact, the establishment of national science bureaucracies very often had the effect of giving scientists more power at the national level and access to more resources. The argument here is not that states would now run and control scientists and science, but that science would be organized nationally, for national benefit, rather than internationally.

Teaching states to fulfill their new role in science quickly became UNESCO's principal science mission, and by 1960 the special Research Organization Unit of the Natural Sciences Department had been established to deal with these tasks.[55] Efforts to establish and expand science policy organizations were undertaken on several fronts. First, following instructions from the Executive Board, the UNESCO field offices organized a series of meetings to promote the idea of science policy and disseminate information about establishing the necessary policy machinery.[56] At the time these meetings took place in 1959 and 1960 in Southeast Asia, Latin America, and the Middle East, very few of the attending countries had science bureaucracies. Only three of the eleven countries at the Latin American regional meeting did; only one of the Middle Eastern countries at the Cairo meeting had such a body.[57] In all

54. This interpretation is compatible with the conclusions of Stephen D. Krasner in *Structural Conflict: The Third World against Global Liberalism* (Berkeley: University of California Press, 1985).

55. The Research Organization Unit was subsequently renamed the Science Policy Division. For more on the early activities of the Research Organization Unit, see Hemptinne, "UNESCO's Role," 244–48.

56. "UNESCO Science Cooperation Offices," *UNESCO Chronicle* 7 (1961): 433–35.

57. "The Development of Science in Southeast Asia," *Nature* 186 (1960): 859–60; "Organization of Scientific Research in Latin America," *Nature* 188 (1960): 1157–58. The

three cases, these were only the first of what became a series of meetings on science policy, for once all states in the region had created the policy machinery, talks continued on how this machinery could be refined and improved.[58]

In addition, UNESCO undertook a series of studies on science policy issues, published as the series Science Policy Studies and Documents. The first four and many of the subsequent studies concern the science policy establishments of individual states and are designed to provide ideas and models to states seeking to establish and improve their own science policymaking. Other volumes in the series treat more general issues of science policymaking, such as the fifth volume, *Principles and Problems of National Science Policies*, (1966) or the sixth, *Structural and Operational Schemes of National Science Policy* (1967). Both of these studies were coupled with meetings of government science officials from member states. The participation of these officials in producing the recommendations of the studies insured that the recommendations were reaching the desired audience. Perhaps most interesting, UNESCO officials would, if requested, come into a country and provide on-site consulting services about how a science policy program might be established there. By early 1966, UNESCO had science policy promotion programs of this kind either completed or underway in fifteen countries and programs to revise existing state science policy bureaucracies along preferred UNESCO lines in several others.[59]

The preferred UNESCO form for a science bureaucracy had two key features. First, the entity making science policy could not also *do* science; it could not also be a research organization. The new science organization could not objectively assess national research priorities when it also had a vested interest in certain lines of research being done in its own labs. It had to be liberated from such conflicts of interest. Second, the science

---

three Latin American countries having science bureaucracies were Argentina, Brazil, and Mexico. Resolutions and Declarations from this seminar are found in UNESCO archives, doc. NS/ROU/36. On the Middle East conference, see UNESCO, *Structural and Operation Schemes of National Science Policy*, Science Policy Studies and Documents, vol. 6. (Paris: UNESCO, 1967); "Science Planning, Development and Co-operation in the Countries of the Middle East and North Africa," *Nature* 189 (1961): 362–63.

58. Results of some the later meetings were later published as part of the Science Policy Studies and Documents series.

59. Science policy establishment missions were complete or underway in Algeria, Congo (Leopoldville), Ethiopia, Guinea, Iran, Iraq, Kenya, Lebanon, Madagascar, Morocco, Senegal, Sudan, Tanzania, Venezuela, and Zambia. Science policy modification or reorganization programs were undertaken in Indonesia, the United Arab Republic, Nepal, and the Philippines, among others.

policy body had to have access to the highest levels of government. It should be a ministerial-level body or should be located close to the seat of power—for example, in the president's office. It should not be subservient to another ministry, such as education or planning, for such an arrangement would seriously limit the organization's independence and prevent the nationwide coordination across all aspects of science that was required. The insistence of UNESCO consultants upon these two features guided the organization's science policy promotion efforts in member states. Its commitment to this particular form of the bureaucracy shows up consistently in its on-site "teaching" activities. The following examples illustrate the ways in which UNESCO succeeded in persuading states to set up science bureaucracies and, more specifically, science bureaucracies of the kind UNESCO preferred.[60]

Lebanon. One of the first places UNESCO officials undertook this kind of science policy consulting was in Lebanon. Because it was one of the first, the Lebanese case became a prototype for UNESCO's later missions. A detailed examination of the case reveals the extent of UNESCO's influence. The head of the Natural Sciences Department actually drafted the enabling legislation for the new bureaucracy while other members of the secretariat staff lobbied relevant Lebanese politicians to get it passed. In doing so, they squelched a conflicting Lebanese proposal for the new bureaucracy, which they considered inappropriate and inadequate.

The starting point for UNESCO's involvement in Lebanon was the regional conference on science planning organized by the Middle Eastern Field Office in Cairo in December 1960. At that conference, Field Office staff members presented reports on the organization of science in various countries of the region. The report on science and technology in Lebanon revealed that Lebanese research lacked any practical orientation and that coordination of research was almost non-existent.[61] However, the report did not have precisely the intended effect. Rather than prompting the Lebanese government to begin organizing and coordinating scientific research, as the Cairo conference had recommended, it prompted the Lebanese Foreign Affairs Ministry to request UNESCO's help in setting up a scientific research *center,* to be part of the University

60. All citations of letters and memoranda in this entire section are from UNESCO Secretariat Registry files, UNESCO archives, Paris. Where documents were assigned file numbers, these are noted in brackets.

61. As described in memorandum by Hemptinne, scientific secretary to the director of the Department of Natural Sciences, to Malcolm S. Adiseshiah, assistant director-general, UNESCO, May 1961 [NS memo 50.085.]

of Lebanon, which could carry out rather than coordinate scientific research in Lebanon in an efficient and effective way.[62] This request was channeled to Yvan de Hemptinne, scientific secretary to the director of the Natural Sciences Department at UNESCO. After reviewing the request, Hemptinne responded that a country like Lebanon did not need more laboratories or research centers; instead it needed coordination of its existing research efforts. He proposed that, rather than sending an expert to set up a research center, UNESCO should send an expert to set up a coordinative science policy body.[63]

Negotiations over which project UNESCO would support, the center to carry out research or the science policy body to coordinate research, ended when the director-general of UNESCO himself, René Maheu, intervened with the president of Lebanon.[64] The new body was to be a national research council that would organize research and make policy about science rather than a research center that would do research. On Maheu's instructions, Hemptinne spent several weeks during the summer of 1961 in Lebanon drafting enabling legislation for this council.[65] Key features of his proposal were that the coordination of research in all scientific disciplines was to be centralized under the council and that the council was under no circumstances to operate any type of laboratory or research facility itself.

The next stage of UNESCO's work involved sending a second science policy expert, Charles Boschloos, to Lebanon to work with the Lebanese to refine and revise the proposed legislation drafted by Hemptinne. The Lebanese, by this time, had formed a National Scientific Commission of their own, whose purpose was to work with UNESCO specialists in designing the new council. In December, Boschloos and the Lebanese com-

62. Described in letter by Fouad Sawaya, director general of national education, Lebanon, to Adiseshiah, 23 May 1961.

63. Memorandum, Hemptinne to Adiseshiah, May 1961 [NS memo 50.085.] Hemptinne also proposes an elaborate three-tiered structure for this coordinative bureaucracy. These proposals were greatly simplified under pressure from F. Karam at the Bureau of Member States (BMS) and from the director-general of UNESCO himself. See memorandum, Karam to José Correa, director of BMS, 5 May 1961 [BMS 80/memo 100]. See also memorandum, director-general of UNESCO [Maheu] to M. V. Kovda, director of the Department of Natural Sciences, UNESCO, n.d. [June or July 1961].

64. Memorandum, director-general of UNESCO [Maheu] to Kovda, n.d. [June or July 1961]. The fact that the director-general of UNESCO and the president of Lebanon were both involved in these negotiations indicates the importance attached to them by both parties. Maheu, in fact, goes on to say in the above-cited memo: "For many reasons, I attach the utmost importance to this project which, in my view, has great value as an example." Translation mine.

65. This proposed legislation is UNESCO archives doc. NS/ROU/7, 8 February 1962.

mission circulated their revised draft of the enabling legislation. It differed in several ways from Hemptinne's draft, notably by weakening
both of what Hemptinne had considered to be the key provisions of the
legislation—that all scientific disciplines were to be brought under
Council jurisdiction and that absolutely no direct involvement in research activities was to be permitted. Hemptinne and other secretariat
members were furious.[66] Boschloos' contract was terminated and elaborate negotiations were undertaken with the Lebanese commission to
push the legislation back onto what secretariat members considered to
be the right track. UNESCO submitted formal comments to the commission on the revised draft, arguing for changes back to the original proposals on these important issues.[67] After several weeks of negotiation,
Hemptinne was permitted to compile a synthesis of the two existing
drafts for consideration by the Lebanese parliament.[68] In it, he included
strong statements about both of his chief concerns while making con-
cessions to the commission's draft on issues of less consequence. The
synthesis proposal was submitted the Lebanese parliament in February
1962. Now the parliament had two alternatives to consider: the
Lebanese commission's proposal and Hemptinne's new revised proposal. To promote his alternative, Hemptinne traveled to Beirut that
spring to answer questions and speak with members of parliament about
the new council proposals. He feared that the commission would produce some new counter-proposal and derail his efforts. To defend
against this possibility, he enlisted the help of the commission's new
president, Joseph Najjar, to keep him informed of any new develop-
ments.[69] In the end, the lobbying efforts by Maheu, Hemptinne, Karam,
Adiseshiah, and others at UNESCO paid off. On 28 August 1962 the

66. See, inter alia, memorandum from Karam to A. K. Kinany, chief, Unit of Arabic-
speaking Countries, BMS, 15 December 1961, and letter from Hemptinne to T. O. P. Lil-
liefelt, permanent resident, Technical Assistance Bureau, Beirut [NS 801/226(40)], 20
December 1961.

67. These comments are contained in UNESCO archives doc. NS/ROU/9, "Commen-
taires de L'UNESCO sur l'avant-projet de loi portant création d'un 'Conseil National de la
Recherche Scientifique' redigé en novembre 1961 par la Commission Scientifique Nationale du Liban," 8 February 1962.

68. UNESCO archives doc. NS/ROU/10, "Avant-projet de loi portant création au Liban:
Synthèse des avant-projets de loi établis par M. Y. de Hemptinne, Chef du Groupe d'or-
ganisation de la recherche scientifique de l'UNESCO et par la Commission Scientifique
Nationale du Liban," 8 February 1962.

69. Letter, Hemptinne to President Najjar, National Scientific Commission, Ecole
Supérieure d'Ingenieurs, Université de St. Joseph, Lebanon, 20 February 1962. Note that
Hemptinne is now head of the new Research Organization Unit (ROU) at UNESCO's Nat-
ural Sciences Department.

Lebanese parliament approved Hemptinne's synthesis proposal for a National Scientific Research Council without discussion.[70]

UNESCO's activities in Lebanon did not stop with the creation of the council. Following passage of the enabling legislation, UNESCO immediately plunged into the task of helping the Lebanese set up the new bureaucracy and ensuring that the Lebanese science policy body headed in the desired direction. Before the end of 1962, UNESCO was recruiting two "experts in the organization of scientific research" to go to Lebanon and draft operating regulations, budgets, and an organization chart for the new Scientific Research Council.[71] UNESCO also conducted external reviews of Lebanese science policymaking at frequent intervals over the next decade, offering suggestions for improvement.[72]

East Africa. Obviously UNESCO's experiences in promoting science policy bodies among its members differed in different countries. Records from one of UNESCO's large science policy campaigns in East Africa during 1967 and 1968 provide some insight into the range of experience of UNESCO consultants. First, consultants did not always spoon-feed the structure of the new science policy bureaucracy to countries as they did in Lebanon. Sometimes the original draft of enabling legislation for the new bureaucracy came from some group within the country, often a ministry of education or a ministry of planning, and was then sent to UNESCO headquarters or to the UNESCO regional office for comments and suggestions.[73] As discussed earlier, however, UNESCO officials had some firm notions about what these science policy bureaucracies should look like and did not let these opportunities to impose their views escape. Most often, the drafts were returned, not just with extensive comments but also with a visit by an expert, who would meet with relevant local officials and

70. Letter, Chafic Moharram, technical counselor to the president of Lebanon, to Hemptinne, 3 October 1962. Hemptinne's enabling legislation specified that the council's budget was not to be less than 1 percent of the state's budget.

71. See, for example, the report by B. K. Blount, deputy director of the British Department of Scientific and Industrial Research and temporary consultant to UNESCO, "Report to the National Research Council of Lebanon," compiled 10 March through 7 April 1964, Lebanon file, Secretariat Registry Files, UNESCO archives.

72. See, for example, unpublished UNESCO reports by P. Piganiol, "Organisation de la politique scientifique au Liban," 1967–1968, and M. Steyaert, "Liban: Politique scientifique national et organisation des recherches oceanographiques," 1968, both in Lebanon file, Secretariat Registry Files, UNESCO archives.

73. It should be noted that even in these cases, UNESCO activities still provided some of the impetus for creating the new bureaucracy. Virtually all of these locally drafted enabling documents cite UNESCO regional science policy conferences (for example, the 1964 Lagos Conference among African countries) as prompting local activity, and most follow conference recommendations to a large extent.

talk about what UNESCO perceived as shortcomings of the country's plan and the organization's proposed remedies.

In 1966, the Ethiopian government, for example, sent a draft of their order on the establishment of a National Research Council to UNESCO's regional office, which forwarded it, along with suggested revisions, to the Science Policy Division staff at headquarters in Paris. Headquarters then sent one of their science policy experts to Addis Ababa to attend meetings of the Drafting Committee for the Research Council Order and to provide information regarding certain aspects of the proposed council's potential activities.[74] A similar course of events took place in Tanzania.[75] Zambian officials, on the other hand, were making good progress toward creating an organization to be called the National Science Policy Board without intervention when UNESCO staff officials discovered their activity. UNESCO consultants immediately inserted themselves into the process, offering advice and suggestions without any direct appeal from the Zambian government.[76]

The obstacles encountered by UNESCO officials in setting up these science bureaucracies also varied from country to country. In Ethiopia, experts complained that creation of the research council was "not very popular" and that those working on the project "seem to be interested in safeguarding those rights and privileges of their institutions that might be delegated to the N.R.C. [National Research Council.] Hence they try to reduce the would-be powers of the N.R.C."[77] In Sudan, UNESCO officials had trouble finding enough qualified scientists even to draft a proposal for the new science policy body, let alone staff it once it was created.[78] In Tanzania, UNESCO officials complained that a general apathy about the entire project prevailed.[79] In Kenya, consultants complained of attempts to subordinate the science policy body to the Ministry of Economic Planning rather than making it part of the president's office and giving it direct access to the highest levels of govern-

74. "Ethiopia," confidential annex I to science policy memorandum 541, I. C. Koupalov-Yaropolk, UNESCO science policy consultant, to A. Matveyev, assistant director-general, UNESCO, 13 April 1967, Secretariat Registry files, UNESCO archives.

75. "Tanzania," annex V to science policy memorandum 541.

76. "Zambia," annex VIII to science policy memorandum 541.

77. "Ethiopia," confidential annex I to science policy memorandum 541.

78. "Sudan," annex VII to science policy memorandum 541.

79. UNESCO consultant Koupalov-Yaropolk described the situation as follows: "The draft Constitution of the National Research Council has been lying for some 14 months in the Ministry of Agriculture. [This] indicates that there are few people really interested in the establishment of N.R.C. or that they do not have influence enough to push this matter forward." "Tanzania," annex V to science policy memorandum 541.

ment.[80] One feature commonly remarked upon by consultants in many countries was the lack of familiarity with the notion of a science policy bureaucracy even in the highest government and science circles, which made it "necessary" for UNESCO officials to spread the word. For example, in Ethiopia consultants were "astonished" to find that they were the first people to present the idea of a national research council to the deans of the Medical, Engineering and Building Colleges at Haile Selassie I University, despite the fact that the vice-chairman of the committee drafting the enabling legislation for the council was the dean of the Faculty of Sciences at the University.[81]

Despite these difficulties, all of these East African states had installed science policy bureaucracies of a type in keeping with UNESCO's guidelines by 1970, within three years of the consultants' initial visits.[82]

IMPLICATIONS

When initially analyzing the data on the creation of science policy organizations, I noted that for the earliest innovators in this area such as the United States and the United Kingdom, demand-driven explanations may be sufficient. UNESCO did not, after all, invent science policy. Rather, it picked up the notion from these successful and powerful states and popularized it. Thus, while the first science policy organizations may have been created in response to domestic demand, subsequent adoptions were strongly influenced by systemic norms promoted by UNESCO. This kind of systemic supply operation differs from simple imitation or mimetic explanations—the more common explanation for diffusion patterns in the organization theory literature—on two counts. First, mimesis is an unmediated process; it locates the impetus for imitative actions in the imitator. In this case, mimesis would claim that each state, looking out at the world of states, decided it wanted a science bureaucracy like the ones created by a few prominent trend-setters. As the foregoing analysis makes clear, this is not what happened. Knowledge of these innovations and assertions of the value of these innovations were *supplied* to

80. See discussion of two key features of UNESCO's preferred form of a science policy making body, above.

81. "Ethiopia," confidential annex I to science policy memorandum 541.

82. Kenya is the exception, since it did not create its own national science policy bureaucracy until 1977. The rationale given by the Kenyans for not creating such a bureaucracy earlier was that they could derive the necessary benefits from an existing East African regional science policy bureaucracy.

states by a third party, UNESCO. Second, mimesis is a process, not a cause. It says nothing about *why* countries would chose to imitate one particular innovation and not others. I have argued that in this case the driving force behind adoption of this innovation is normative—that states adopted these bureaucracies because of a new understanding of necessary and appropriate state behavior rather than any functional need. Positive evidence for the effects of norms is always difficult to provide, which is one reason such explanations are often treated as residuals. Here, I cite rhetorical shifts in discourse about the organization of science which reflected conceptual shifts that coincide with the behaviors described. This positive evidence, coupled with the failure of alternative explanations, provides a strong case for the role of norms.[83]

Internationally generated normative pressures for state change are not confined to science policy. Similar studies have documented such normative influences in shaping bureaucracies and policies in the areas of education, employment, social welfare, citizenship, and weapons procurement. International norms shape state constitutions and support the continuation and spread of the political form of the state itself against other competing forms of political organization.[84] I stress international normative determinants of state structure because I believe they have

83. In their analysis of the spread of municipal reforms across U.S. cities at the turn of the century, Tolbert and Zucker provide a similar explanation of a diffusion process. Their interpretation is as follows: "As an increasing number of organizations adopt a program or policy, it becomes progressively institutionalized, or widely understood to be a necessary component of rational organizational structure. The legitimacy of the procedures themselves serves as the impetus for the later adopters." Pamela Tolbert and Lynne Zucker, "Institutional Sources of Change in the Formal Structure of Organizations: The Diffusion of Civil Service Reform, 1880–1935," *Administrative Science Quarterly*, 28 (1983): 35.

84. On education, see John Meyer, Francisco Ramirez, Richard Rubinson, and John Boli-Bennett, "The World Educational Revolutions, 1950–1970," *Sociology of Education* 50 (1977): 242–58; on employment and economic development generally, see John Meyer and Michael Hannan, eds., *National Development and the World System* (Chicago: University of Chicago Press, 1979); on social welfare, see David Strang and Patricia Mei Yin Chang, "The International Labor Organization and the Welfare State: Institutional Effects on National Welfare Spending, 1960–80," *International Organization* 47 (1993): 235–62; on citizenship, see Yasemin N. Soysal *Limits of Citizenship: Migrants and Postnational Membership in Europe* (Chicago: University of Chicago Press, 1995); on weapons procurement, see Dana P. Eyre and Mark C. Suchman, "Status, Norms, and the Proliferation of Conventional Weapons: An Institutional Theory Approach," in Peter J. Katzenstein, ed., *The Culture of National Security* (New York: Columbia University Press, 1996); on constitutions see John Boli, "World Polity Sources of Expanding State Authority and Organization, 1870–1970" in George M. Thomas et al., eds., *Institutional Structure: Constituting State, Society, and the Individual* (Newbury Park, Calif.: Sage, 1987), 71–91; on state longevity, see Strang, "Anomaly and Commonplace in European Political Expansion: Realist and Institutionalist Accounts," *International Organization* 45 (1991): 143–62.

been overlooked or underemphasized by other scholars. I do not wish to suggest that these are the only determinants of state structure. International norms create pressures for isomorphism among states; they by no means create equifinality. Variations in local conditions, both material and social, as well as international coercion have a great deal of influence. But the single case focus of most studies of state change tends to emphasize the unique and local at the expense of the similar and shared and obscures processes that systemic analyses such as this one can reveal.

Appendix to Chapter Two: Data and Sources

SCIENCE POLICY ORGANIZATIONS

Definition

In its *World Directory of National Science Policy-making Bodies*, UNESCO defines these organizations as those whose "central policy making function [is] . . . national level . . . planning, organization, or co-ordination of scientific and technological activities. Organizations such as Ministries or Departments of Science and Technology, National Research Councils, and Academies of Science, as well as other bodies with similar overall responsibilities, have thus been included in the new Unesco directory; bodies whose responsibilities are limited to specific sectors of the economy or particular fields of science and technology have, on the contrary, not been included."[85]

Two ambiguities arise in the coding. The first concerns generalized state planning agencies whose responsibility is to plan all aspects of the economy. If these plans include science, do they qualify as science policymaking bodies? The 1984 directory is silent on this point, but the earlier directories of the 1960s specifically exclude entities with such general responsibilities. I have done the same in requiring that these organizations have science as their central concern. The second ambiguity concerns the status of national academies of science. For theoretical reasons, made clear in the chapter, I am interested only in state organizations. However, not all academies are part of the state apparatus. In the United States, for example, the National Academy of Sciences is a private professional society. However, in many countries academies enjoy some amount of state support, and in the Soviet Union and Soviet-style states academies were constituted in such a way as to

---

85. UNESCO, *World Directory of National Science Policy-making Bodies*, viii. See also the definition in the earlier directories.

make them difficult to distinguish from the state apparatus. In such cases, the active policymaking and advising role played by academies might very well be considered the first state science policymaking organization.

To determine whether or not academies should be counted as state science policy bureaucracies I defer to the UNESCO Science Policy Studies and Documents series written by officials of the countries under study. If they presented their academy as their first science policy organization, as Cuba did, then it is coded as such. If they treated the academy as a fore-runner of the "real" science policymaking apparatus, as the USSR did, then it is not coded.

Date of Creation of Initial Science Policy Organizations

These data were obtained from UNESCO's Science Policy Studies and Documents series. Most items in that series are analyses of science policy activity in a region or UNESCO member country and usually include a brief history of science policy activity there. Often countries have experienced a series of science policymaking organizations as different governments have reorganized their bureaucracies. Ambiguity about which of these might be the first science policymaking organization is resolved by deferring to the nationals of the country or region in question who authored these studies. This is clearly preferable to some coding that allows UNESCO bureaucrats to designate the first organization which qualifies as a science policy body.

SCIENCE DATA

Data on the number of scientists and engineers involved in research and development (SEINRD) and the amount of spending on R&D as a percentage of GDP in the year science policy organizations were created (RNDGDP) were obtained from the UNESCO *Statistical Yearbooks*. Not all countries collect science data in all years. LDCs in particular are sporadic in the collection of science data. Where SEINRD and RNDGDP figures are not available for the year of creation, the figure for the closest year available is used. In two cases (Chile and Tanzania), R&D spending figures are unavailable; thus the RNDGDP analysis has been done on a sample of 42 rather than 44 countries.

The *Statistical Yearbooks* contain extensive definitions of "scientist," "engineer," and "research and development" used in compiling their data. For purposes here, it is worth noting that all of these figures, including R&D spending, are for *both* public and private sectors.

67

The number of scientists and engineers per thousand population, shown in Figure 2, is obtained by dividing SEINRD figures by country population as given in the same *Statistical Yearbook* for the adoption year.

DEVELOPMENT DATA

GDP per capita in constant 1980 U.S. dollars (GNPCONCP) is used as a rough measure of development. These data are not available in constant dollars of the same base year for the relatively large span of years under study here; they have been calculated from the International Monetary Fund's *International Financial Statistics Yearbooks*. Where necessary, conversions from one base year of $U.S. to $U.S. (1980) have been made using producer price indexes found in the *Statistical Abstract of the United States*. Populations figures are taken from the UNESCO *Statistical Yearbooks*. For countries not members of the IMF, gross *national* product per capita figures for the relevant years from the U.S. Arms Control and Disarmament Agency's *World Expenditures and Arms Trade* (Washington, D.C.: U.S. Government Printing Office) are substituted.

SECURITY DATA

Defense spending as a percentage of gross national product (DEFGNP) in the year of science policy creation is used as a measure of perceived security threat. These figures are obtained from *World Military Expenditures and Arms Trade* when available for the necessary years. In cases where science policy organizations were created prior to 1963 (when the Arms Control Agency began collecting these data) DEFGNP figures are obtained from national statistical abstracts.

Defense spending is only a rough measure of perceived security threat since there is a host of domestic reasons why states may spend on defense, having to do with maintaining stability of governments. However, since these distortions generally increase rather than decrease defense spending, they should make us suspicious of false positive findings rather than false negatives. Thus, if the data revealed a correlation between high defense spending and the creation of science policy institutions, we would want to look further at our defense figures. The fact that even with these distortions states create science institutions at consistently low levels of defense spending supports rather than undermines my hypotheses.

CHAPTER THREE

Norms and War:
The International Red Cross
and the Geneva Conventions

International relations scholars have tended to think of war as a Hobbesian state of nature. In war, above all other situations, we should be able to treat states and soldiers as self-interested utility-maximizers simply because in times of war the most basic survival interests are at stake. In fact, however, war is a highly regulated social institution whose rules have changed over time. Interstate war could not even be conducted if survival were the paramount concern of soldiers and other individuals because in war the requirements of state survival and personal survival directly conflict. Soldiers may not fight without some other social value or interest such as honor, nationalism, or political ideology. It is social values that give war a purpose, that define its meaning and make it worth fighting. Social norms also govern the way in which states and soldiers fight. Notions of chivalry and codes of conduct for the warrior are as old as war itself. Some of these norms clearly contribute to fighting efficiency and survival—norms of unit solidarity, for example. Other rules of war are less easily understood outside of a larger social and normative context.[1]

In this chapter I examine the origins of one prominent and apparently expanding collection of rules of warfare—the Geneva Conventions, which specify a variety of humanitarian protections for both wounded soldiers and noncombatants that warring states must guarantee. Signatories agree to provide these protections even to soldiers and civilians of

---

1. John Keegan provides extensive empirical evidence concerning the cultural nature of warfighting in *A History of Warfare* (New York: Vintage, 1994).

the states with whom they are at war. Why would states want to protect enemy soldiers and foreign civilians in the middle of a war? The practical importance of these norms is fairly obvious; conformance to humanitarian norms makes the world a safer and more pleasant place to live. Theoretically, however, humanitarian norms, more than most kinds of norms, challenge central notions about sovereignty and the organization of international politics in important ways. Three possible explanations for the origin of the Conventions are suggested by conventional approaches to state behavior that take interests for granted. I find little evidence to support these explanations. The alternative explanation developed in this chapter focuses on the role played by a few morally committed individuals and the organization they built, the International Committee of the Red Cross (ICRC), in promulgating and transmitting humanitarian norms.

Since its founding in the mid-nineteenth century, the ICRC has tried to protect individuals from suffering caused by state violence in four ways: (1) it has sought to ensure humane standards of treatment and neutrality status for noncombatants, particularly medical personnel, the wounded, and civilians; (2) it has sought to provide aid to prisoners of war and facilitate their return; (3) it has sought to provide humanitarian aid to non-state forces during civil conflicts; and (4) it has sought access to and humanitarian treatment for political prisoners. Its primary means of accomplishing these goals have been the establishment of national relief societies (what are now the national Red Cross societies in most countries) and international treaty guarantees concerning each of these four areas of humanitarian behavior (what are now known as the Geneva Conventions.)

ICRC efforts in each of these areas were contested by states at the time they were proposed as an infringement on state war-making powers or sovereign rights. Each has now been established with some degree of normative authority in the system. In answering the research question of how these norms became established, my analysis focuses on the role of the ICRC in codifying the first of the four types of norms—standards of treatment and neutrality status for noncombatants, particularly the wounded and medical personnel. Historically this was the first area of interest of the ICRC; in fact, it was this issue that inspired the creation of the Committee. Subsequent efforts to establish concern for other norms within the ICRC have been strongly colored by the worldview and moral code elaborated in this early period of its history.

Unlike those in the previous case, the outcomes here were very much the intended result of policy entrepreneurs.[2] Henry Dunant's reforms were not filtered through a large, preexisting intergovernmental bureaucracy. Rather, the IO implementing change is nongovernmental and was designed specifically for the purpose. These two facts have made the ICRC a very different kind of teacher from either UNESCO or the World Bank, both in the case under review here and in the 130 years since.

HUMANITARIAN NORMS AND INTERNATIONAL RELATIONS THEORY

The fundamental difficulty with asserting humanitarian norms in a world dominated by states is that humanitarian values are premised on a worldview not easily accommodated within the principles and rights associated with state sovereignty. In a states system, the unit of concern is the state; individuals are recognized and categorized only in their relationship to the state, primarily as citizens or aliens. By contrast, the humanitarian worldview asserts that individuals have status and worth independent of their relationship to states. By asserting that human beings have rights and value simply by virtue of their humanity, humanitarians create a set of normative claims that compete with the claims made by states. They assert that states do not have unlimited rights to pursue and defend their national interests; rather, that pursuit must be tempered by respect for the well-being of individuals. Thus, to the degree humanitarian claims succeed, they constrain states, circumscribing their sovereignty and their free exercise of power.[3]

2. For an early discussion of political entrepreneurs, see Terry M. Moe, *The Organization of Interests: Incentives and the Internal Dynamics of Political Interest Groups* (Chicago: University of Chicago Press, 1980), chap. 3. For a more recent analysis directly related to the case discussed here, see Ethan Nadelman's discussion of "transnational moral entrepreneurs" in "Global Prohibition Regimes: The Evolution of Norms in International Society," *International Organization* 44 (1990): 479–526.

3. It should be emphasized that, while the claims of sovereignty and human rights are in tension, they are not diametrically opposed. States, after all, gain some legitimacy by claiming to serve the welfare of individuals within them. In fact, one of the classic moral justifications given by practitioners of realpolitik for their policies is that protection of the national interest is the best way to protect the individual within the state. See Hans Morgenthau, *Politics among Nations*, 5th ed. (New York: Knopf, 1973). This attempt at reconciliation does not completely solve the problem, however. The realist claim is still fundamentally one that sets the welfare of citizens above aliens and even justifies abuse of the latter in the protection of the former. Humanitarians, by contrast, are concerned primarily with individuals and would argue that the good of the state should be pursued within the context of humane treatment of all individuals, regardless of citizenship.

The humanitarian claims of the ICRC are of special significance because they have focused on the aspect of state power most central to the essence of sovereignty itself—the state use of violence. It is precisely the control over the use of arms that states guard most jealously. In the classic Weberian definition, the defining element of the state is its monopoly on the legitimate use of force within a given territory.[4] ICRC claims for the protection of individuals from the effects of state violence are claims that the exercise of that essential monopoly must be limited. Claims that states must restrain their use of violence in wartime should be particularly difficult for humanitarians to establish. War is presumably a time when states' vital interests, even survival, are at stake. One would not expect policy makers or generals to take on burdens making protection of those vital interests more difficult. But they do. Compliance with ICRC requirements that states provide enemy wounded with medical treatment equal to that provided for their own soldiers is one example. From a rationalist or realpolitik perspective there is no good reason to treat someone in enemy uniform needing medical attention. That person might still turn out to be dangerous, and, even if the combatant is not a threat, why invest scare resources in aiding an enemy?

Several explanations suggest themselves as possible causes of this behavior. First, states might be prompted into humane treatment of enemy wounded and medical personnel by the simple hope of reciprocity—treating and repatriating enemy wounded in the hope that their wounded will be similarly treated and returned. This hypothesis presupposes that states, in fact, have some reason to place significant value on their wounded. They could do this for two reasons, each of which suggests a further cause for states' interest in the wounded.

States might care about the wounded for purely instrumental military reasons, such as wanting their trained soldiers back so they can fight another day. It would, after all, be much cheaper and easier to reintegrate veterans than to train raw recruits. Alternatively, states might care about humane treatment of the wounded for domestic political reasons. Following the logic of Immanuel Kant, one might expect the democratizing forces at work in Europe in the nineteenth century, when the ICRC was founded, to create powerful constraints on leaders of democratic states to protect their citizen-soldiers from harm.[5] Establishment of humani-

4. Max Weber, *Economy and Society*, ed. Guenther Roth and Claus Wittich (New York: Bedminster, 1968), 56.
5. Immanuel Kant, "Perpetual Peace" (1795); reprinted in *On History*, ed. and trans. Lewis White Beck, The Library of Liberal Arts (Indianapolis: Bobbs Merrill, 1963), 85–135.

tarian laws of war and relief societies to aid the wounded would offer those leaders powerful political tools to legitimate their governments.

The following analysis will show that, while all of these reasons may have played some role, none is sufficient as an explanation for the formation of the ICRC and the ratification of the first Geneva Convention. Early applications of the Geneva Convention in wartime were unilateral, undermining the reciprocity argument. Military and medical technology in the 1860s was such that the wounded were unlikely to be fit for combat anytime during the conflict (if, indeed, they were ever fit again), undermining the utilitarian argument. Finally, the earliest and most enthusiastic supporter of the Red Cross and the Geneva Convention was Prussia, one of least democratic states in Europe. Britain, perhaps the most democratic, was one of the most recalcitrant.

In addition to failing on the facts, all these explanations suffer from misidentification of the underlying impetus for these events. These explanations identify states as the prime movers behind the origins of the ICRC and the Convention. However, the ICRC and the Convention were not state initiatives. They are the product not of state action, but of action by private individuals. Individuals, not states, formed the organization, which in turn drew up the Convention and persuaded states to adhere.

ORIGINS OF THE INTERNATIONAL COMMITTEE OF THE RED CROSS AND THE FIRST GENEVA CONVENTION

The catalyst for the founding of the ICRC lies in the experiences of one individual, Henry Dunant.[6] Dunant (1828–1910) was a Genevese-Swiss banker who, for a combination of personal and professional reasons, happened to be in Lombardy in 1859 during the Italian wars of

6. Surprisingly little historical work has been done on the International Committee of the Red Cross. Much of what does exist has been written and published under the auspices of the ICRC itself. By far the best single source is the Committee's own two-volume history written by Pierre Boissier and André Durand in the late 1970s and early 1980s. See Pierre Boissier, *From Solferino to Tsushima: History of the International Committee of the Red Cross,* (Geneva: Henry Dunant Institute, 1985) and André Durand, *From Sarajevo to Hiroshima: History of the International Committee of the Red Cross* (Geneva: Henry Dunant Institute, 1984). The Committee's monthly magazine, *Revue internationale de la Croix-Rouge,* occasionally contains historical pieces and published a larger-than-average number of these around the time of the organization's centennial in 1963–1964. Other sources used to construct the following account include Martin Gumpert, *Dunant: The Story of the Red Cross* (New York: Oxford University Press, 1938); Alexis François, *Le berceau de la Croix-Rouge* (Geneva: Librairie A. Jullien, 1918); Henri Coursier, *The International Red Cross* (Geneva: ICRC, 1961).

independence.[7] Immediately following the engagement between French and Austrian forces at Solferino on 24 June, Dunant arrived in the nearby town of Castiglione to find thousands of wounded soldiers from both sides flooding the town with virtually no medical care in sight. At that time, the French army marched with less than one physician per thousand men; its artillery did not have a single doctor. The situation among the Austrians was no better. There were no medical supplies or equipment to be had; even food and water were scarce.[8]

Confronted with this scene of chaos, Dunant could have fled. Instead, he threw himself into relief work—cleaning wounds, dispensing water and food, canvassing the local community for what supplies could be had. The experience had a profound effect on Dunant and prompted him to publish an account of his experiences entitled *A Memory of Solferino*.[9] In addition to providing a lively and detailed description of Dunant's experiences, the book contains a proposal for change, a remedy for the horrors Dunant encountered. Dunant proposed that relief societies staffed by qualified volunteers be set up to care for the wounded in wartime. Further, he proposed that these volunteer relief societies be officially recognized in an international agreement. Building an organization in peacetime, Dunant argued, was the best insurance of adequate care for all wounded after hostilities had broken out.[10]

Dunant published his work at his own expense and sent copies to members of ruling families, influential politicians, philanthropists, and newspaper publishers. The book was an instant success. It went through three printings in the first four months, attracted notice in most of the influential newspapers of Europe, and became a subject of conversation in the salons.[11]

7. For background on Dunant prior to his involvement in the ICRC, see Boissier, *Solferino to Tsushima*, 7–16; Gumpert, *Dunant*, 3–31.

8. Total casualties from the battle at Solferino have been estimated at 6,000 dead and 42,000 wounded. That would make it the bloodiest battle since Waterloo. The number of those wounded brought into the town of Castiglione, whose peacetime population was about 5,000, was estimated at 9,230 by the physician in charge. Gumpert gives a figure of 6,000 wounded to be treated by only two doctors. By contrast, there were roughly four veterinarians per thousand horses in the French army. Boissier, *Solferino to Tsushima*, 20–23; Gumpert, *Dunant*, 46.

9. 1862; reprint, Geneva: ICRC, 1986. The French title, *Souvenirs de Solferino*, has also been translated as *Recollections of Solferino* in other editions.

10. Dunant, *A Memory*, 115–28.

11. Reviews of the first and third editions of *A Memory* which appeared in the *Journal de Genève* are reprinted in "Au temps de 'Congrès de Genève,'" *Revue international de la Croix-Rouge*, no. 425 (May 1954): 370–73. The influential *Journal des Débats* (15 Feb. 1863) also gave the book high praise. Discussions appearing in other publications are noted in François, *Le berceau*, 117.

Dunant received a flood of correspondence from readers, among them the author Victor Hugo; the philosopher Ernest Renan; the peace activist Frédéric Passy; Surgeon-General A. Bertherand; Prince Alexander of Hesse; the king of Holland; the grand duke of Baden; Marshall Randon, the French minister of war; Ferdinand de Lesseps, the celebrated builder of the Suez Canal; and Florence Nightingale.[12]

Among those impressed by the book was a lawyer and fellow citizen of Geneva, Gustave Moynier. Moynier was chairman of the Geneva Society for Public Welfare, a private institution devoted to philanthropy and social progress. After reading *A Memory of Solferino*, he sought out Dunant and proposed that the Society for Public Welfare take up Dunant's suggestion for the formation of relief societies in a practical way. At the Society's next meeting a committee of five men was set up to investigate Dunant's proposals. These five shortly became the International Committee to Aid the Military Wounded, which would later be called the International Committee of the Red Cross.[13] The original five members of the Committee were Moynier; Dunant; General Dufour, commander of the Swiss army and former military instructor of Louis Napoleon; and two physicians, Louis Appia and Theodore Maunoir. Appia was a military physician of wide experience who had, in fact, been near Solferino at the same time as Dunant. Maunoir was a civilian surgeon whose recommendation for the position seems to have been the great respect he commanded among his peers.

After two initial meetings, the Committee decided that the best way to achieve its goal of creating relief societies in each country was not to try and do this themselves but to convene an international congress of interested and influential delegates from each country, who would return

---

12. Gumpert, *Dunant*, 104; Boissier, *Solferino to Tsushima*, 40–43; François, *Le berceau*, 119. Not all of this correspondence was laudatory. Randon, for example, was incensed and viewed the account as an attack on France and the French military. Nightingale, while supportive of Dunant's exposé of medical conditions in the military, was not enthusiastic about his proposed solution. She shared the view that her government later voiced at the Geneva conferences, that care for the war wounded was a government responsibility, not a task for volunteers. Boissier, *Solferino to Tsushima*, 41–42. The grand duke actually sent money, as well as a letter, to help Dunant set up his relief societies. *Journal de Genève* (19 Mar. 1863), reprinted in "Au temps de 'Congrès' ": 373–74. For more detail on Dunant's contacts in the salons of Paris and elsewhere, see Gumpert, *Dunant*, chap. 6. Dunant submitted much of this correpondence to the Committee after it was formed and notes it in his minutes of Committee meetings. These are reprinted in "La fondation de la Croix-Rouge: Quelques documents essentiels," *Revue international de la Croix-Rouge*, no. 530 (Feb. 1963): 56–72.

13. The change in name occurred in 1880: "La fondation de la Croix-Rouge."

home and implement Dunant's proposals.[14] Anticipating resistance to their plan from military commanders, who had already expressed reservations about the notion of volunteers cluttering up battlefields and confusing military operations, the Committee decided at its first meeting that all relief societies must gain official government recognition and be made subject to the orders of military commanders. This meant that participation by philanthropists was not sufficient; the conference had to attract delegates from governments, particularly from military commands.[15]

To ensure attendance by delegates from as many countries as possible and to ensure that those delegates were sufficiently influential in their home countries, the Committee undertook what would now be called a publicity campaign to interest possible participants in their project. As Maunoir put it, it was necessary to "maintain *une agitation*, if one can put it that way, so that our views will be adopted by everyone, high and low, from the sovereigns of Europe to the people themselves."[16] In fact, the strategy adopted for this *agitation* was largely a top-down one. The Committee would first contact governments and others in power to ensure their support for the formation of a national relief society. Once in place, the national society would be responsible for publicity for its cause in that country and the development of mass support for the project.[17]

Dunant became the principal executor of this *agitation* among elites. He began by attending a session of an international statistical congress in Berlin, the fourth section of which was concerned with comparative health and mortality statistics and was attended overwhelmingly by civilian and military doctors. In addition to an address to this group, Dunant made personal contact with scores of delegates, promoting his ideas and inviting influential people to attend the upcoming conference in Geneva. By the end of the conference he had provisional acceptances

14. Minutes of 25 August 1863 meeting of the Committee, ibid., 66. The Committee's invitation to the Congress is reprinted in Jean Pictet, "Centième anniversaire de la première convention de Genève," *Revue international de la Croix-Rouge*, no. 548 (Aug. 1964): 384–85.

15. It was the military man on the Committee, General Dufour, who proposed this requirement. See the minutes of the first two meetings of the Committee, 17 February and 17 March 1863, reprinted in "La fondation," 59–65.

16. As transcribed in Dunant's minutes of the Committee's first meeting, 17 February 1863, reprinted in "La fondation," 58, trans. mine.

17. Minutes of 17 February and 17 March meetings, ibid. It should be noted, though, that the activities of the Committee received regular press coverage in a number of publications, thereby bringing the Committee's project to the attention of a wider public. For a few examples, see the reprints from *Journal du Genève* reprinted in "Au temps du 'Congrès.'"

from representatives of Sweden, Denmark, Hanover, Bavaria, Mecklenburg, Prussia, Spain, and Italy.[18]

Dunant then traveled to Potsdam and was received by King Wilhelm I and Crown Prince Friedrich as well as the Prussian minister of war, the court physician, the army physician and the minister of the interior. While in Prussia, Dunant also made contact with the official representatives of Russia, Spain, Saxony, Bavaria, and Norway, each of whom promised to take up Dunant's cause with their respective governments. He later traveled to Saxony and secured support from the king there, then to Vienna, Bavaria, Darmstadt, Stuttgart, and Karlsruhe. He wrote letters to Lord Grey, Britain's minister of war, and to France's commissary-general, Baron Darricau, who persuaded Louis Napoleon to allow him to send a representative to the Geneva conference.[19]

Dunant's efforts paid off at the October 1863 conference in Geneva. Attendance at the conference surpassed his and the Committee's expectations. Thirty-one delegates from sixteen countries and three philanthropic societies responded to the invitation. Represented were Austria, Baden, Bavaria, Britain, France, Hanover, Hesse, Italy, the Netherlands, Prussia, Russia, Saxony, Spain, Sweden, Switzerland, Württemberg, the Order of St. John of Jerusalem, the Neuchâtel Social Science Society, and the Society for Public Welfare of the Canton of Vaud.[20] Virtually all these governments and societies had been contacted personally by Dunant. Most of the representatives were military physicians, usually heads of the military medical corps of their countries.[21]

18. Dunant's letters to Moynier during this congress are explicit discussions of networking strategy in which Dunant reports his progress and assigns to Moynier the job of securing representation from countries he (Dunant) has not yet contacted. See letters, Dunant to Moynier, reprinted in "Notes et documents: Conférence internationale pour la neutralisation du service de Santé Militaire en Campagne," *Revue International de la Croix-Rouge* 425 (May 1954): 424–28. It was while attending this conference that Dunant added the notion of neutrality to his proposals for volunteer relief societies. He did this without the knowledge and consent of the rest of the Committee, causing considerable consternation when reports of his activities reached Geneva. Gumpert, *Dunant,* 114–16; Boissier, *Solferino to Tsushima,* 61–67; also letters, Dunant to Moynier, reprinted in "Notes et Documents," 424–28.

19. Dunant also traveled to France before the conference, primarily to help set up a French relief society, but also to persuade various French elites to use their influence on other, more recalcitrant, potential participants. Minutes of 13 March 1864 meeting of Committee, reprinted in "La fondation," 70; Pictet, "Centième anniversaire," 381.

20. This is the list given in Boissier, *Solferino to Tsushima,* 70.

21. For a complete list of participants and their titles, see description of the conference in *Journal du Genève,* reprinted in "Au temps de 'Congrès,' " 398–403; also Boissier, *Solferino to Tsushima,* 70.

Prior to the conference, the Committee had drafted a convention, which contained details of the organization of relief societies, for the assembled delegates to consider. After some discussion and amendment, the proposals considered were the following. Each country was to establish a national relief society whose mission would be to provide aid to war wounded regardless of nationality. The societies were to be private organizations staffed by volunteers and funded by private donations.[22] They were to seek recognition from national governments and could act in armed conflict only when invited to do so by the national military. All volunteers were to wear a white armband with a red cross so that they could easily be identified. In addition, neutral status was be extended to all medical personnel, including all volunteers, both from relief societies and from the civilian population at the battle site, as well as to the wounded themselves.[23]

These provisions did not sail through the conference unopposed. The French and the British, in particular, opposed the very concept of volunteer relief societies. Neither wanted to see civilians on the battlefield meddling in what should properly be military affairs. The French distrusted the competence and integrity of these volunteers. They did not believe the societies would ever be able to supply themselves adequately with food, clothing, and medicines amid the difficulties of war. Civilians suddenly thrown into the chaos and horror of war were unlikely to perform effectively; they would be paralyzed by the sight of blood and unable to survive in the privations of war. Protecting these civilians would thus become one more strain on an army already engaged in combat. Further, the French delegate voiced fears that the relief societies would

22. One of the recommendations of the conference was that governments should "extend their patronage" to the new societies and "facilitate as far as possible the accomplishment of their task" (quoted in Boissier, *Solferino to Tsushima*, 81.) This opened the door to government contributions to the new organizations, but government funding was never expected to constitute a large portion of the societies' resources.

23. The inclusion of neutrality among the proposals was particularly controversial. Dunant managed to place it on the conference agenda against the wishes of the other four members of the Committee, who felt that asking for neutral status was going too far and that states would never agree. As it turned out, delegates to the 1863 conference were much more concerned about the proposed relief societies themselves than about neutral status. It was not until the negotiations over the drafting of the 1864 Geneva Convention that neutrality again emerged as controversial. In that case, states agreed to accord neutral status to military medical personnel and the wounded only, not to relief society volunteers. Although the 1874 Brussels declaration accorded neutral status to volunteers, the declaration did not have the force of law since it was never ratified. Volunteers were not formally granted neutral status until the 1949 revision of the Convention. See Boissier, *Solferino to Tsushima*, 61–83, 112–21, 293.

attract volunteers from the lower classes who could not be relied upon to maintain orderly conduct or to refrain from plundering the dead and wounded.[24] The British objection was simply that these societies were superfluous in the British army. Following the horrors of Crimea and the efforts of Florence Nightingale, the British military medical services had been completely overhauled and much expanded. They were now fully adequate, the British claimed, to care for military wounded in any conflict and did not need civilian assistance to accomplish their task. In the British view, care for military wounded was a state obligation. If other states copied the British reforms, the Committee's relief societies would not be necessary.

The principal supporters of the Committee's proposals were the German states, particularly Prussia, which took exception to the British position, arguing that it made no economic sense for the state to maintain a standing medical corps large enough to meet all military eventualities. Further, it was pointed out that in Germany there was a long tradition of the Knights Hospitalers, a noble order of unquestioned integrity, providing voluntary aid to the war wounded without undue interference in military affairs or collapse under the strain of battle.[25]

In the end, the Prussian arguments, supported by other German states, swayed the delegates and the conference voted unanimously to adopt the Committee's proposals. The conference was adjourned and the delegates sent home with two tasks: to start the work of setting up relief societies in the home countries and to persuade their governments to accept and sign an international agreement recognizing (1) the neutrality of military and relief society medical personnel, civilian volunteers, the wounded, hospitals, and ambulances; and (2) some uniform emblem to distinguish these personnel, hospitals, and ambulances.

Relief societies were formed quickly in Württemberg, Oldenburg, Prussia, and Belgium, but by March 1864 it was clear that the societies were encountering serious opposition in important European states. In the Netherlands, the society was rejected because relief of war wounded was regarded as a state responsibility.[26] The Austrians argued that they already had a relief society: the Austrian Patriotic Society for Aid to

24. This is discussed in Boissier, *Solferino to Tsushima* and in John Hutchinson, "Medical Opponents of the Red Cross," *Proceedings of the XXXIId International Congress on the History of Medicine*, Antwerp, 3–7 September 1990: 239–46.

25. Boissier, *Solferino to Tsushima*, 73–76; Gumpert, *Dunant*, 128–30; *Journal de Genève*, reprinted in "Au temps du 'Congrès,'" 386–87.

26. Boissier, *Solferino to Tsushima*, 89.

Wounded Soldiers, War Widows, and Orphans.[27] Efforts to form a Russian society were thwarted by the minister of war, Milutine, who refused to allow volunteers onto the battlefield. The British continued to oppose founding of any such society on the grounds that their War Office had already taken on this responsibility and was carrying out these duties effectively. Marshall Randon also continued his opposition to the societies in France, and it was only because Dunant spent several months in the salons of Paris pushing his cause and eventually gained an audience with Louis Napoleon himself (by using a letter of introduction from Dufour) that Randon was circumvented and the society's proponents given official state sanction.[28]

To implement the second part of the conference's resolutions, the Committee began drafting an international agreement in which neutrality status and a distinctive emblem were explicitly recognized. There was no precedent for a diplomatic convention of this kind. Previously, laws of war had been based solely on customary usage and, to a lesser extent, on legal opinions. The Committee's initiative was the first step in constructing a treaty-based law of war.[29] To obtain signatures for the new convention, the Committee persuaded the French and Swiss governments to sponsor an international conference at which states would hammer out details of the treaty and formally accept it. Many states were not enthusiastic, as their earlier treatment of the relief society proposals suggests. In the end, however, a group of seventeen states, very similar to the group of states attending the 1863 conference, convened in Geneva in August 1864.[30] Only Austria, Bavaria, and the Vatican refused the invitation outright, Austria because it considered its Patriotic Society adequate for all requirements, and the latter two because of Catholic distaste for the Geneva location of the conference. Brazil, Mexico, Greece, and Turkey

27. In fact, the Patriotic Society proved impotent in the face of actual war responsibilities. Among the difficulties it encountered was lack of communication with other relief societies or the Austrian military, such as would have been afforded a Red Cross society. Consequently, following the Austro-Prussian War (1866), a Red Cross society was formed in Vienna and granted recognition by the ICRC.

28. *Journal de Genève*, reprinted in "Au temps du 'Congrès,'" 391–96. For more on Dunant's efforts to found the French relief society, see, "Chronique: Henry Dunant et la Croix-Rouge française," *Revue international de la Croix-Rouge*, no. 545 (May 1964): 260–66.

29. Boissier, *Solferino to Tsushima*, 113.

30. Lists of attendees vary slightly among sources. The official list from ICRC archives is: Baden, Belgium, Denmark, France, Great Britain, Hesse, Italy, the Netherlands, Portugal, Prussia, Saxony, Spain, Sweden, Switzerland and Württemburg. Pictet, "Centième anniversaire," 385–86. As a result of some bureaucratic confusion, the Russian delegate arrived after the conference was over. Gumpert, *Dunant*, 154.

did not attend but sent messages of endorsement. The United States participated only as an observer. The U.S. delegate, Charles Bowles, was representing not the government generally, but the U.S. Sanitary Commission, which was busily revamping military medicine among the Union forces in the American Civil War.[31]

The principal provisions of the Convention agreed upon by the delegates were as follows.

- Ambulances, military hospitals, medical personnel, and the administrative, transport, and quartermasters's staff which supports these would all have neutral status.[32]
- In the event of enemy occupation, these neutral personnel would have the right to continue to carry out their functions. When they chose to return to their units, this return would be facilitated by occupying forces.
- Hospital materials captured could be retained by the occupying forces; ambulances could not.
- Civilians living near the battlefield who provided aid to the wounded should be respected and remain free. Generals of belligerent powers had a duty to notify these civilians of the neutrality such humane conduct would confer.
- Wounded and sick combatants should be collected and cared for. Those recovered, if unfit for further service, must be repatriated. Those fit for service should be repatriated on the condition that they not take up arms again for the duration of hostilities. Evacuation parties conducting these repatriation operations should be neutral.

31. Gumpert provides an extensive reprint of Bowles's fascinating report on the conference. *Dunant* 157–70. For more on the U.S. Sanitary Commission see the two part series in the *Revue international de la Croix-Rouge*, nos. 532–33 (Apr., May 1963), "Le premier effort moderne de codification du droit de la guerre: Francis Lieber et l'Ordonnance Générale no. 100." Boisser denies that Dunant and later Moynier were influenced by foreign models, American or otherwise, in their original conception of the Red Cross and the earliest meetings of the Committee. I have found no evidence to the contrary. Given the backgrounds and experience of the two, which were not in the military or in medicine, Boissier's claim seems plausible. However, the importance of models from previous European or foreign experiences clearly rose as the movement matured and more people with wider experience became involved. Bowles certainly believed that he and the Sanitary Commission's example were having an effect at the 1864 Geneva Conference. Gumpert, *Dunant* 157–70; Boissier, *Solferino to Tsushima*, 163–65.

32. One source of controversy at the conference was whether the volunteers of the relief societies should enjoy neutral status. The treaty does not mention them. The Prussian delegates pushed strongly for explicit recognition of the volunteers in the treaty. The French had been instructed by Randon not to sign anything conferring neutrality on the volunteers. The vague language about "medical personnel" in the treaty was designed to placate both parties.

- Personnel, hospitals, and ambulances enjoying neutral status should wear the emblem of neutrality, a red cross on a white background.

Not all delegates had been sent to the conference with full powers to sign the agreement. Consequently, only twelve states signed at the close of the convention on 22 August 1864: Baden, Belgium, Denmark, France, Hesse, Italy, Netherlands, Portugal, Prussia, Spain, Switzerland, and Württemberg. By the end of 1866, however, twenty states had signed. By 1868, Russia and the Vatican had adhered. Thus, within four years, virtually every state in Europe was a signatory to the Convention, plus some of the most important extra-European states—the United States and Turkey.[33]

EARLY APPLICATIONS OF THE GENEVA CONVENTION IN WARTIME

The first test of the Geneva Convention came in 1866, when fighting broke out between Prussia and Austria over control of the German Confederation. At this time, only Prussia was a signatory to the Convention; Austria had continually refused to accede despite intercession by the French ambassador on the part of the Committee.[34] The Prussian response in this case was to apply the Convention unilaterally. Prussia maintained unilateral application despite Austrian refusal to return captured Prussian doctors. Similarly, Italy, a signatory to the Convention, applied its provisions unilaterally when it joined Prussia in the attack on Austria.[35] The other early conflict in which one side was party to the Convention and the other was not was the Sino-Japanese War of 1894. In that case, too, the Japanese chose to apply the protections of the convention unilaterally.[36]

33. A list of signatory states and their date of signing through 1907 can be found in Pictet, "Centième anniversaire," 401–2. Within this time there was a second conference at which additions to the original Geneva Convention were agreed to. The most notable of these were extension of Geneva principles to naval warfare and provisions that parties to the Convention would compile lists of dead, wounded, and prisoners for exchange with other belligerents.

34. Gustave Moynier, president of the ICRC, noted that the Austrian refusals showed a complete lack of comprehension of what the Convention was about since they focused on Austria's perceived self-sufficiency to handle its own war wounded rather than on issues of neutrality. Boissier, *Solferino to Tsushima*, 178.

35. Ibid., 182–86.

36. The Sino-Japanese war was also the first application of the Geneva Conventions to naval warfare as required by the 1867 amendments.

The Franco-Prussian War (1870) was the first conflict in which both parties were adherents to the Convention. What was notable in the case was the way in which both used compliance or noncompliance as a propaganda tool in the war. The very fact that the Convention was so used indicates the degree of normative authority it already carried in international public opinion.[37] Overall, the Prussians were better able to observe the Convention than the French simply because the French relief societies were too few and too disorganized to do their job. The French societies had not been able to publicize the meaning of the red cross armband and neutral status for medical personnel adequately among the military ranks and civilian population. Several ICRC and relief society workers from neutral countries complained of being treated as spies by French unfamiliar with the Convention. Not surprisingly, the Prussians published many similar stories.

Later conflicts posed important issues for the Committee, and it was through these that the scope of the Convention's protections for individuals in wartime was gradually increased. The Balkan Wars (1875–1878), in which Herzogovina, Bosnia, and Bulgaria rebelled against the Turks, are especially notable as precedent setters. First, they raised the question of applying the Geneva Conventions in cases of civil war. Initially, the Committee announced that these protections applied only in *interstate* conflicts.[38] Later, however, it changed its mind, stating that humanitarianism is a "profession of faith" and a "moral code"; it cannot, therefore, be optional sometimes and compulsory at others.[39] This conflict was also the first case in which Red Cross principles—principles the Committee had hitherto understood as the "Christian principles"—were applied outside the Christian West. One result of this was to clarify

37. The ICRC has always been explicit that it considers public opinion to be the only tool of enforcement of the Geneva Convention(s). One potentially interesting research project suggested by this study would be to disaggregate the "public" and explore whose opinion matters, when and how. In the early days of the Red Cross movement it is clear that elite opinions and support were essential in founding the relief societies and gaining signatures for the Convention. Later, as the movement grew, the relief societies expanded, and public awareness of the Convention(s) increased, a broader spectrum of opinion probably became important.

38. This was explicitly decided at the second meeting of the Committee, 17 March 1863. See minutes reprinted in "Fondation de la Croix-Rouge," 63. It was also decided at this meeting that Red Cross principles would be applied only to European conflicts. This decision, too, was obviously revised.

39. The earlier Carlist insurrection in Spain provided some precedent for this decision. In that case, the national Spanish Red Cross Society decided that foreign combatants should not be receiving greater protection than the country's own citizens, and on this basis, they decided to act. Boissier, *Solferino to Tsushima*, 298.

the universal nature of Red Cross humanitarian claims on states; *all* states could and should conform to Geneva principles, which were compatible with all religious beliefs.[40] Hand in hand with this, however, went a concession to religious and cultural diversity—the admission of the Red Crescent as an alternative symbol for the humanitarian relief societies.[41] Finally, the Balkan Wars provided the first case in which civilian refugees were explicitly recognized as victims of war and eligible for Red Cross protection. Rather than simply being a society to aid the war wounded, the Red Cross had now expanded its mandate to provide relief for all suffering caused by what it called "man-made disaster."

THE RED CROSS AND MILITARY MEDICINE

During the first twenty years of the ICRC's history, military medicine underwent some remarkable changes, which were both consequential for and caused, in part, by the Red Cross itself.[42] Enumerating the qualities needed for volunteer relief work in 1867, ICRC Committee members Moynier and Appia emphasized respectability and impartiality; they said nothing about medical knowledge.[43] Neither did Dunant in his initial call for creation of the relief societies.[44] And, indeed, given the state of military field medicine, further qualifications were hardly necessary. It did not require extensive training to teach volunteers to hold a patient down on the operating table while his leg was being amputated, the saw still

40. This step was particularly important in light of the strongly Christian revivalist motivations of Dunant. For more on Dunant's religious beliefs and how it affected his work, see Gumpert, *Dunant*, especially chap. 1. See also the discussion below of the role of morally committed individuals. Note, too, that Moynier, president of the ICRC for 48 years, described the Red Cross as a product of progressive "Christian civilization" and attributed the success of the Red Cross movement to the growing influence of Christianity. Gustave Moynier, *Les causes du sucèss de la Croix-Rouge* as quoted in Boissier, *Solferino to Tsushima*, 344.

41. It became apparent during this conflict that the Red Cross flag was sufficiently provocative to Turkish troops that it had the opposite effect from that intended. Instead of protecting those under it, the flag made them targets. Boissier quotes some rather horrific accounts of treatment of Red Cross personnel during the conflict at the hands of Muslim Turks. Boissier, *Solferino to Tsushima*, 303–12.

42. Ibid., 297–332.

43. Ibid., 316. Social respectability and integrity of the volunteers also was a key issue in the 1863–1864 debates over the founding of the relief societies. As was discussed previously, the French delegate to the 1863 Congress, Dr. Boudier, was concerned about the class of people who might volunteer for such relief work.

44. The only qualifications mentioned are "sincerely philanthropic motives." Dunant, *A Memory*, 117.

dripping with blood from the previous operation. Neither was it difficult to learn to wash a wound with water from the local stream or to apply already-used lint and bandages. Certainly this was the extent of Dunant's own activities at Solferino and the situation had changed little through the Franco-Prussian War.

By the 1880s, however, such methods were no longer tolerated. The work of Louis Pasteur had made sterilization routine practice in military hospitals. Surgeons increasingly demanded trained nurses and medical orderlies to safeguard the hygiene of their patients and carry out increasingly complex procedures. In fact, it was very often Red Cross personnel themselves who introduced these changes into military hospitals. The resulting change in mortality rates was extraordinary. In the Serbo-Bulgarian War (1885), only 2 percent of the 6,000 wounded Serbians died. Hospital gangrene all but disappeared, the amputation rate plunged, and the success rate on those amputations rose.

In addition to changes in medical technology, two changes in weapons technology also influenced the change in mortality—the introduction of steel-jacketed small caliber bullets and the repeating magazine. The military advantages of these innovations were clear. Reducing the calibre of the bullet from 11mm to 7mm allowed soldiers to open fire at a range of 2,000 meters. The repeater system increased the rate of fire from four shots per minute to twenty. The medical consequences were at least as great as the military consequences. Greater firepower increased the number of wounded but it also changed the character of the wounds. The narrower, high-speed bullet penetrated with greater force but, paradoxically, also caused less lethal damage. With greater velocity, these bullets did not lodge in the body but penetrated completely and created relatively small holes when they entered and left. Infections became less common with fewer gaping wounds. Excessive hemorrhaging and bone shattering became rare. The need for amputations decreased.

As a result of this, the relationship between the wounded, military hospitals, and the army changed. In the 1860s, the wounded were a military write-off. With the existing state of military medicine, the number of wounded who could be saved at all was not large; the proportion of those who would be fit for duty within the duration of the conflict was negligible. By the mid-1880s, however, military hospitals were recycling troops back into the army in significant numbers. Thus, by the time the military and medical technology combined to make protection of the wounded a material asset to armies, the Red Cross movement and the Geneva Convention were already firmly established. However, at the time states were making the decision to adhere to the convention and found relief societies, the military utility of treating the wounded was negligible.

MORALITY, INDIVIDUALS, AND INTERNATIONAL RELATIONS THEORY

The foregoing analysis makes clear that none of the three above-stated hypotheses about why states would agree to provide humanitarian aid to the wounded provides a sufficient explanation for the origin of the ICRC and the Geneva Convention. Unilateral application of the first Convention undermines arguments about reciprocity as states' chief motive. Early support for ICRC activities from less-democratic states, such as Prussia, and recalcitrance by the most democratic state, Britain, cuts against Kantian arguments about pleasing mass publics as a causal motive. Technological innovations in munitions and medicine do not coincide well with the timing of state adherence to the Conventions and formation of Red Cross societies. The societies were promoters of military medical change, not results of it. All these arguments miss the real causal forces at work by focusing on states as the important actors. What is essential in the origin of the ICRC and the Geneva Convention is the role of a few morally committed private individuals—individuals without government positions or political power—and the elite networks they were able to use to build an international organization. Neither of these has received much attention from international relations scholars. The state-centric analysis dominating the field has made it difficult to recognize that private individuals with no formal political standing might have significant influence.[45] Furthermore, realism's rejection of morality as a

45. The epistemic community literature is beginning to make inroads in this direction. However, the group of elites active in the founding of the ICRC would not qualify under Peter Haas's definition of an epistemic community as "a network of professionals with recognized expertise and competence in a particular domain and an authoritative claim to policy-relevant knowledge within that domain or issue-area." Peter Haas, "Introduction: Epistemic Communities and International Policy Coordination," *International Organization* 46 (1992): 3. The ICRC group lacked both specialized knowledge and competence of any obvious kind. What the group did have, however, is the set of principled beliefs that can create an agenda for action. For a discussion of the ways in which international moral norms and principled beliefs are constructed and disseminated by "issue networks" of philosophers, lawyers, religious leaders, educators and government officials, see Robert McElroy, *Morality and American Foreign Policy* (Princeton: Princeton University Press, 1993) chap. 2. A related but less specific argument can be found in Michael Walzer, *Just and Unjust Wars: A Moral Argument with Historical Illustrations* (New York: Basic Books, 1977). Kathryn Sikkink provides an excellent study of this phenomenon in the human rights field in "Human Rights, Principled Issue-Networks, and Sovereignty in Latin America," *International Organi-*

significant force in world politics provides few tools for understanding people like Henry Dunant or the widespread ethical convictions he harnessed.[46]

A social constructivist approach to politics allows us to make sense of principled concerns, morality, and individual action. The discussions surrounding the adoption of the Geneva Conventions and subsequent compliance were not about interests and advantage. They were discussions about duties, responsibility, and identity. They were discussions about appropriateness. Dunant framed his appeal in terms of the responsibilities of Christian gentlemen and civilized nations. Leaders justified decisions to sign and comply on the basis of religious and moral duty borne by civilized nations. Citizens embraced the conventions for similar reasons.

Principled concerns about war-making and war-fighting are the rule, not the exception as realists might have us believe. War engages some of the most fundamental issues of morality and conscience. It raises questions about treatment of other human beings at the most fundmental level, for it involves killing large numbers of them. Warmaking is permeated by norms and social structure. This is as true now as it was of the Christian gentlemen of Dunant's era. Nina Tannenwald's work on no-first-use norms for nuclear weapons illustrates this, as does Richard Price's work on taboos against biological and chemical weapons.[47] The bulk of military activity following the Cold War has been intervention to save civilian populations of little or no strategic importance in places like Somalia and Cambodia.[48] These discussions are, again, not about interest and advantage. They are about responsibility and duty. The international

---

zation 47 (1993): 411–41, as does Jack Donnelly in "International Human Rights: Regime Analysis," *International Organization* 40 (1986): 599–632.

46. For more on Dunant's religious beliefs, see Gumpert, *Dunant,* chap. 1. Gumpert also notes that, prior to his involvement in the Red Cross, Dunant was a founding member of the YMCA. See also Coursier, *The International Red Cross,* 16. One indicator of Dunant's altruistic commitment to his cause is the fact that he spent large amounts of his own money promoting it and eventually bankrupted himself in the service of the Red Cross. As a result, he virtually disappeared from the organization after 1867 and was actually believed to be dead until a Swiss journalist discovered him in a hospice in Heiden in 1895. Gumpert, *Dunant,* chaps. 14 and 19.

47. Richard Price and Nina Tannenwald, "Norms and Deterrence: The Nuclear and Chemical Weapons Taboos," in Peter Katzenstein, ed., *The Culture of National Security: Norms and Identity in World Politics* (New York: Columbia University Press, 1996); Richard Price, "A Genealogy of the Chemical Weapons Taboo," *International Organization* 49 (1995): 73–103; Nina Tannenwald, "Dogs That Don't Bark: The United States, the Role of Norms, and the Non-Use of Nuclear Weapons in the Post-WWII Era," Ph.D diss., Cornell University, 1995.

48. Martha Finnemore, "Constructing Norms of Humanitarian Intervention" in Katzenstein, ed., *The Culture of National Security.*

community is said to have a "duty" and "responsibility" to prevent these disasters. But responsibilities and duties are created by normative understandings and social structures. Without society and community, they do not exist. Without an understanding of the social fabric that creates these perceptions of responsibility and duty, we cannot understand state action.

CHAPTER FOUR

Norms and Development: The World Bank and Poverty

The notion of economic development as a goal of states is often treated as unproblematic in contemporary political discourse. Wealth is treated as a constant goal of states, and "development" in the twentieth century lexicon is the means to wealth. However, the concept of development leaves open questions about both the ends of the development process (develop into what? wealth for whom? wealth for what end?) and the means of the process (develop how?). States' understandings of the ends and means of development have shifted over time. The focus on raising GNP as the preeminent development goal, which prevailed in the 1950s and 1960s, has been expanded with additional concerns about income distribution, poverty alleviation, environmental preservation, cultural integrity, and human rights. The focus of development strategies, the means to development, has similarly shifted from concerns about capital accumulation, foreign exchange, and construction of large industrial projects such as dams and power plants to concerns about small farmers, renewable resources, and the provision of social services in urban areas.[1]

In one of these shifts in development goals, poverty alleviation became a defining feature of development in the late 1960s and 1970s. Before 1968, poverty received scant attention in international development institutions, academic development writings, and national development plans. By the mid 1970s, it had moved front and center in all three are-

1. For an excellent, comprehensive examination of the changing nature of development and its effects, see Arturo Escobar, *Encountering Development: The Making and Unmaking of the Third World* (Princeton: Princeton University Press, 1995).

nas of development work. Furthermore, poverty moved from being a condition of states to a condition of people. To the extent that poverty was discussed in the international development community prior to the 1970s, the discussion was about "poor countries"; beginning in the early 1970s, the poor were widely understood to be individual human beings. States were disaggregated in these new development policies and the poor were targeted *within* states. What caused this shift? There was no significant change in the numbers or condition of the poor during this short period. Nor was there any widespread political change that empowered the poor in LDCs and allowed them to demand attention from national and international development bureaucrats. Nor does there appear to be any sudden rise of powerful, organized philanthropic interests in aid-donor countries who were pressing for new development policies that would target poor populations.

The rise of poverty as an essential element of development makes sense, however, when viewed as a normative shift promoted by an international organization. This shift in development goals was a result, not of domestic political changes within states, but of a change in understandings of norms and the development process that took place at the international level. Making poverty alleviation an essential component of development redefined what it was that states were supposed to do. Previously, states were simply supposed to be engines of growth. Development equaled industrialization, so states were supposed to "develop into" capital accumulators and planners of infrastructure investment. Now states were also supposed to be guarantors of welfare. They were supposed to "develop into" places where not only did national and average per capita income grow, but the distribution of those gains was such that all individuals within the state could be assured of meeting "basic human needs." As in the previous cases, an international organization, the World Bank, played a central role in promulgating and revising these development norms in the international system.[2] Under Robert McNamara, the Bank's influence, its visibility, and its credibility among development experts made it an effective proselytizer for poverty concerns. Its organizational structure was particularly important

---

2. Unless otherwise specified, the terms "World Bank" and "the Bank" are used in this chapter to denote the entire "Bank Group" including the International Bank for Reconstruction and Development (IBRD), the International Finance Corporation (IFC), and the International Development Association (IDA). For a description of the various components of the Bank Group, see Robert L. Ayres, *Banking on the Poor: The World Bank and World Poverty* (Cambridge: MIT Press, 1983), chap. 2.

in this case. While the impetus to do something about poverty came largely from an individual leader, McNamara, the precise form of the poverty alleviation strategies pushed by the Bank was a product of the structure of the organization rather than anything inherent in the poverty norms themselves. Aid to small farmers and urban site-and-services provision became equated with poverty alleviation and succeeded where other proposals failed because these were strategies that met the organizational needs of the Bank.

This chapter examines three hypothetical sources for the shift in development goals and strategies—states (both LDCs and industrialized nations [INs]), development experts, and international organizations—in light of available evidence. I find that states contributed very little to the incorporation of poverty alleviation into development. With a few exceptions, national governments in LDCs saw little political benefit in diverting resources to their poor populations and sometimes actually resisted these efforts. Industrialized donor states similarly had no particular interest in helping the poor in LDCs and certainly did not make it a political issue or priority. A small group of development experts in universities and multilateral lending organizations did provide intellectual justification for elevating poverty as a concern, but the expert community as a whole was divided over the desirability of this move. This division created a permissive environment for change, largely by providing a critique of the neoclassical orthodoxy's ability to "trickle down" benefits; however, the concerned experts had neither a widely agreed-upon alternative to offer nor a power base from which to push that alternative. It was the Bank, enjoying a peculiar combination of structural features and led by a visionary president, that "sold" poverty alleviation as an essential component of development policy to its member states through a mixture of persuasion and coercion. There are parallels between this articulation of poverty alleviation as an international social concern and an analogous domestic phenomenon in the nineteenth century in which national governments began identifying poverty as a social problem to be dealt with, rather than an inevitable fact of life. The normative and philosophical implications of these domestic changes have been widely explored. Those of us studying international politics and development might learn something from that literature.

The chapter does not argue that the World Bank or anyone else has succeeded in alleviating poverty in the developing world. Assessments of the success of development efforts have been undertaken by a large number of experts and critics. My purpose here is, instead, to try to understand more clearly what this massive development effort *is* that consumes so many national and international resources, what those involved in it are trying to do, how their goals change over time, and why they change. In addition, I do not argue that the World Bank invented poverty as a concern. Concerns about global poverty had been expressed in a variety of quarters prior to McNamara's appearance at the Bank. What McNamara and the Bank did was to institutionalize this concern, to make it an inextricable part of what development was all about. Before McNamara, being "developed" meant having dams, bridges, and a (relatively) high GNP per capita.[3] After McNamara, being developed also required the guarantee of a certain level of welfare to one's population.

Poverty as a Concern before 1968

Prior to World War II, concern with poverty across national borders was largely the province of religious and private philanthropic groups.[4] Governments might occasionally supply relief aid in response to a natural disaster, famine, or war—an example is Herbert Hoover's aid efforts following World War I including his famine relief to Soviet Russia from 1921 to 1923—but they did not concern themselves with chronic structural poverty in other countries until after 1940.[5] Following the Great Depression and World War II, states begin to articulate a more internationalist sense of community that included poverty alleviation. When Roosevelt spoke of "freedom from want . . . everywhere in the world" in his Four Freedoms speech justifying the American war effort in 1941, he

3. Edward S. Mason and Robert S. Asher, *The World Bank since Bretton Woods* (Washington, D.C.: Brookings Institution, 1973), 152; Ayres, *Banking on the Poor,* 2–3.

4. For a discussion of the history of international responses to poverty, see Marilyn I. McMorrow, "Not by Bread Alone: Deprivations, Subsistance Rights, and Obligation in International Society," Ph.D. diss., Princeton University, 1991, chap. 4. For a related history of the rise of foreign aid, see David H. Lumsdaine, *Moral Vision in International Politics: The Foreign Aid Regime, 1949–1989* (Princeton: Princeton University Press, 1993), especially chap. 6.

5. It might be argued that socialist governments, specifically Soviet Russia, are exceptions to this. However, the Soviets were concerned more with revolution and political power than poverty alleviation (since the former, in their view, were requirements for the latter). In addition, espousal of these concerns by the Soviets did not result in widespread institutionalization of an antipoverty norm. See Robert W. McElroy, *Morality and American Foreign Policy* (Princeton: Princeton University Press, 1992), chap. 3.

clearly expressed a responsibility for economic conditions in other states.[6] The Atlantic Charter reiterated the "freedom from want" objective. After the war, claims about international obligation and intent to alleviate poverty became more universal and more explicit largely as a result of United Nations activity. The Universal Declaration of Human Rights, adopted by the General Assembly in 1948, claims that all human beings have "the right to a standard of living adequate for the health and well-being of [themselves] and of [their] families, including food, clothing, housing, and medical care." The Covenant on Economic, Social and Cultural Rights, adopted by the General Assembly in 1966, reaffirmed these rights and elaborated some of them.[7]

These expressions of concern were not, however, connected to the foundation of the World Bank or any other development effort immediately following the war. The concept of development at that time was not explicitly linked to poverty. The lack of connection is clear from the Bretton Woods discussions, which structured the postwar economic order, and from the way in which the Bank was founded. While the Bank's Articles of Agreement do mention (but do not emphasize) assisting countries in raising standards of living, they do not mention or target poor countries in particular, nor do they mention any kind of guarantee of minimum standards as does the Universal Declaration of Human Rights. Rather, they emphasize productivity, investment, capital accumulation, growth, and balance of payments. Development itself received little attention in the years immediately following the war and was not a major concern at the Bretton Woods conference. The World Bank set up at Bretton Woods was designed primarily to rebuild Europe. Harry Dexter White's original proposal for the Bank called it the "Bank for Reconstruction."[8] The term "development" was added to the title only later in the conference, when E. M. Bernstein (a colleague of White's in the U.S. Treasury) pointed out to White that the Bank needed a more permanent function and suggested that that function be development. Bernstein

6. As Lumsdaine points out, it is doubtful that Roosevelt really envisioned massive capital flows to Asia and Africa for development purposes when he made this speech, even though this kind of foreign aid is implicit in the logic of his statements. Lumsdaine, *Moral Vision*, 202.

7. Note, however, that only about half of the states in the world are signatories to the Covenant and that the United States is not a signatory. McMorrow, "Not by Bread Alone," chap. 4 provides an ethical analysis and critique of the Covenant.

8. White was assistant secretary of the U.S. Treasury and head of the U.S. delegation to Bretton Woods. He and John Maynard Keynes, head of the British delegation, were the architects of the agreements reached at the conference.

later wrote that he "used this term without being aware that it would become of importance in the future."[9]

Including development in the title of the new institution did not mean that the founding donor countries were suddenly concerned with poor countries or poor people in those countries. In the view of John Maynard Keynes, who was chairman of the Commission on the Bank at the Bretton Woods conference: "Twenty-one countries have been invited which clearly have nothing to contribute and will merely encumber the ground, namely, Colombia, Costa Rica, Dominica, Ecuador, Salvador, Guatemala, Haiti, Honduras, Liberia, Nicaragua, Panama, Paraguay, Philippines, Venezuela, Peru, Uruguay, Ethiopia, Iceland, Iran, Iraq, and Luxembourg—the most monstrous monkey-house assembled for years. To these might perhaps be added: Egypt, Chile and (in present circumstances) Yugoslavia."[10] Even the representatives of LDCs seemed unconcerned about development. Only the Mexicans put forward any kind of proposal to focus the new Bank's efforts on development issues. That proposal was supported only by Cuba and Colombia and was rendered inconsequential by Keynes. LDC governments at Bretton Woods tended to view themselves more as "new raw material producing nations" than as countries with development problems and certainly not as poor countries or countries with large poor populations for whom the international community should take some responsibility. LDC country proposals at the conference centered around stabilizing prices in commodities markets; they did not mention poverty.[11]

As European reconstruction got firmly underway in the late 1940s, the attention of industrialized states began to turn to economic issues in LDCs. It was in the fifties and early sixties that bilateral foreign aid programs were created and multilateral development lending via the World Bank (and later, the International Finance Corporation [IFC], the International Development Association [IDA], and regional development banks) was extended to LDCs.[12] During these two decades, a period in

9. As quoted in Gerald M. Meier, *Emerging from Poverty: The Economics That Really Matters* (New York: Oxford University Press, 1984), 12. The fact that Keynes, the chairman of the Commission on the Bank at Bretton Woods, was more interested in the establishment of the International Monetary Fund than the Bank did nothing to elevate development's standing at the conference.

10. Ibid., 11.

11. Ibid., 12–14.

12. The World Bank's first loans were all to European countries and were for reconstruction. The Bank's first development loan was made in 1948 to Chile for two small projects. See Ayres, *Banking on the Poor*, 1. On the origins of bilateral foreign aid, see John

which large numbers of new and increasingly poor countries were coming into being, development assistance was offered to more and poorer countries. Furthermore, loans and aid were increasingly being offered on easier terms and thus were becoming more available to the poorest countries. In 1960, the IDA—the "soft money" window of the World Bank—opened for business with the express purpose of offering loans to countries that were having difficulty meeting the more stringent credit requirements of the Bank proper.[13] Similarly, efforts were made by donor countries to increase the concessionary components of bilateral assistance.[14]

Thus, development activity moved into the areas of the world where the poor were, and the terms of development assistance improved somewhat. However, the "development" activity that was being undertaken with these resources was not poverty alleviation as that activity was subsequently conceived; nor was it understood as poverty alleviation by those who were undertaking it. Development, during these years, was understood to mean increasing GNP or, perhaps, GNP per capita. Increasing GNP, in turn, meant industrialization, and the obstacle to industrialization was capital accumulation. The proper aim of states, and of development, was to promote savings (often through protection against imports), channel investment toward industrialization and, where possible, secure external aid. The development projects undertaken by states in this period were large industrial infrastructure projects, such as dams and highways, designed to have large secondary industrialization-promotion effects.[15] This development orthodoxy was

---

White, *The Politics of Foreign Aid* (New York: St. Martin's Press, 1974) 1–33, 195–227; Lumsdaine, *Moral Vision*, especially chap. 2. On the origins of the IFC and IDA, see Mason and Asher, *The World Bank*, 79–82. On the origins of the regional development banks, see John White, *Regional Development Banks: The Asian, African and Inter-American Development Banks* (New York: Praeger, 1972) 40–51, 91–102, 140–50, and United States Library of Congress, Congressional Research Service, Foreign Affairs Division, *The United States and the Multilateral Development Banks* (Washington, D.C.: USGPO, 1974).

13. Mason and Asher, *The World Bank*, chap. 12.

14. OECD, *Development Cooperation: Efforts and Policies of the Members of the Development Assistance Committee, 1975 Review* (Paris: OECD, 1975).

15. There is an extensive body of writing on the development economics of the period and the intense debates about policy choices within the general development framework. For overviews of development economics in this period, see Meier, *Emerging from Poverty*, chap. 6; John P. Lewis and Valeriana Kallab, eds., *Development Strategies Reconsidered* (New Brunswick, N.J.: Transaction Books, 1986), chap. 1; Mason and Asher, *The World Bank*, 481–87; J. H. Adler, "The World Bank's Concept of Development—An In-House *Dogmengeschichte*," in Jagdish N. Bhagwati and Richard S. Eckaus, eds., *Development and Planning: Essays in Honour of Paul Rosenstein Rodan* (Cambridge: MIT Press, 1973), 30–50. For exam-

widely held. It permeated academic economics circles and the emerging discipline of development economics.[16] It underlay the national development plans formulated by state planning ministries, the staffs of which were often educated by the same academic economists.[17] It dominated thinking in such multilateral lending agencies as the World Bank.[18]

Within this development orthodoxy, poverty was not a visible concern. The approach was not opposed to poverty alleviation in any way. To the extent that anyone thought about poverty, they thought about the salutary effects of GNP growth for all. But mostly they simply did not think about it. Poverty is almost never discussed in the academic literature of the period. It does not even receive lip service in most of the national development plans, and it had virtually no impact on multilateral lending policies or practices.[19] Thus, it is not the case that poverty alleviation was always an integral part of development policies—that before the early 1970s people tried to address poverty problems through growth strate-

ples of writings from this period about development goals and indicators of success, see United Nations, Department of Economic Affairs, *Measures for the Economic Development of Under-Developed Countries* (New York: United Nations, 1951), and United Nations, Conference on Trade and Development, *The Measurement of Development Effort* (New York: United Nations, 1970). These two reports bracket this period nicely. While the second is much more detailed than the first in its econometric measures, both unequivocally focus on savings, investment, and industrialization. Neither mentions poverty.

16. Meier, *Emerging from Poverty*, chap. 6; Lewis and Kallab, eds., *Development Strategies Reconsidered*, chap. 1; Mason and Asher, *The World Bank*, 481–87.

17. For example, see, Jagdish N. Bhagwati and Padma Desai, *India: Planning for Industrialization* (New York: Oxford University Press, 1970); Robert Muscat, *Development Strategy in Thailand: A Study of Economic Growth* (New York: Frederick A. Praeger, 1966); J. P. Pangestu, *Economic Planning Experience in Indonesia* (Singapore: University Education Press, 1971); Mahbub ul Haq *The Poverty Curtain: Choices for the Third World* (New York: Columbia University Press, 1976); Ghana, Planning Commission, *Seven-year Plan for National Reconstruction and Development, Financial Years 1963/4–1969/70* (Accra: Office of the Planning Commission, 1964); Indonesia, Department of Information, *Development: Summary of Indonesia's First Five-Year Development Plan, April 1, 1969 to March 31, 1974* (Djakarta: P.T. Garda, 1969); Nigeria, *Federal Government Development Programme, 1962–68* (Lagos: Federal Printing Division, 1962); Honduras, Committee of Nine, Alliance for Progress, *Evaluation of the National Plan of Public Investments, 1963–1964*, Joint Bank/Fund Library, 1963, mimeograph; Thailand, National Economic Development Board, *The National Economic Development Programme, B.E. 2504–2506–2509 (1961/2–1966)* (Bangkok, 1961).

18. Mason and Asher, *The World Bank*, 481–87.

19. In fact, Mason and Asher's 25-page index to their 900-page history of the World Bank does not have a single entry for "poverty." Despite the 1973 publication date, this history was written to honor the 25th anniversary of the Bank in 1971 and thus ends just as the shift discussed here begins in the Bank. Richard Webb, who is writing on poverty for the World Bank History Project, counted only three mentions of the word in the 900 page text. Mason and Asher, *The World Bank*; Richard Webb, personal communication, 9 June 1993.

gies and subsequently decided to target poverty directly. If this were the case, there would be some discussion of poverty and some data collection to find out how well growth strategies were doing at alleviating it. There is none.

This is not to say that no one cared about poverty before 1968. World poverty may have been a concern of individuals and of some nongovernmental organizations. It may have been implicit in the principles articulated in constructing the postwar international order.[20] It may even, occasionally, have inspired some social democratic governments in Europe in the fashioning of their foreign aid policies.[21] But poverty alleviation did not become an explicitly articulated and internationalized goal of states and multilateral governmental agencies until after 1968. Similarly, poverty alleviation did not became an integral part of development and the discipline of development economics until this time. It was simply not part of the development effort.[22]

This changed in the late 1960s and early 1970s. By the late 1970s, everyone involved in development was talking, writing, and structuring policies about poverty issues. Academic treatises were being published, international conferences were being organized, national development plans were reoriented, and international aid efforts were retargeted. Data began to be collected on the impact of development efforts on poor populations, and these results became the object of intense scrutiny. The goal of poverty alleviation became institutionalized as part of the international development effort. The question is: what caused this change?

SOURCES OF CHANGE: HYPOTHESES

Three possible sources of change suggest themselves. First, and most obviously, the new focus on poverty may have come from states. Poor LDCs might have pushed for this shift, as this is where most of the world's poor reside and where the impacts of poverty are felt most acutely. Alternatively, industrialized states might have pushed for this

20. McMorrow makes this argument in "Not by Bread Alone," chap. 4.

21. Lumsdaine makes this argument in *Moral Vision*, 115–27, 143–81.

22. In his examination of cognitive processes within the Bank, Babai calls this poverty shift "a new hierarchy of objectives" and similarly emphasizes that it was not present in development efforts prior to 1970. Donald Babai, "Between Hegemony and Poverty: The World Bank in the World Economy," Ph.D. diss., University of California, Berkeley, 1984, 390.

shift. They, after all, have the resources to actually do something about poverty, as they control the flows of both bilateral and multilateral aid to LDCs. Some reconfiguration of domestic political interests that empowered the poor in LDCs or gave political access to philanthropic groups in industrialized countries could have resulted in a shift in state policies.

Second, the impetus for change may have come from development experts—development economists, engineers, and consultants who plan and execute development projects. The growing literature on epistemic communities has shown the political importance of such groups of experts in a wide variety of settings and issue areas.[23] Here we would expect to see new, poverty-centered ideas about development percolating up from academic and intellectual circles. These experts could change policies of states either by persuading key policymakers or by colonizing pieces of the government apparatus.[24]

Third, international organizations such as the World Bank, regional development banks, or UN agencies might have played a critical role. While IOs are dependent in many ways upon their member states for funds and support, numerous scholars have argued that they can and do play an independent role in international politics. IOs may have resource bases independent of states (as does the World Bank, which raises its funds for lending in private capital markets). They may have expertise superior to that of many states (as the various banks have over many LDCs), and they may be the beneficiaries of "slack" in the principal-agent relationship between them and their member states. Of these IOs, the World Bank immediately suggests itself as a focus of attention for several reasons: (a) it is the largest multilateral lender to developing states; (b) in addition to the dollar amount of its lending, its actions have important signaling effects to private lenders and donor governments providing development assistance; (c) it serves important facilitating and coordinating functions by brokering the participation of lenders and donors in consortia for development aid packages; (d) it has a highly regarded cadre of experts on its professional staff making

23. For examples, see Peter Haas, *Knowledge, Power, and International Policy Coordination*, special issue of *International Organization* 46 (1992): passim.

24. Emanuel Adler provides a case of persuasion in "The Emergence of Cooperation: National Epistemic Communities and the International Evolution of the Idea of Nuclear Arms Control," *International Organization* 46 (1992): 101–45. Peter Haas's work on the Mediterranean clean-up illustrates the colonization of state bureaucracies by experts. Peter Haas, "Do Regimes Matter? Epistemic Communities and Mediterranean Pollution Control," *International Organization* 43 (1989): 377–403.

decisions about the allocation of that money; and (e) it is global in scope (as opposed to the regional development banks). In addition, the Bank's role as a broker of ideas and a socializer has been suggested elsewhere.[25]

If LDCs were the impetus for the focus on poverty, one would expect to see these governments pushing donor countries and multilateral development banks to redirect their aid packages and lending operations; one would see LDCs using public forums such as the UN to publicize the cause of the poor and press for more and redirected aid to poor populations. Temporally, one would expect LDCs' development efforts and national development plans to show this commitment to poverty alleviation before donor states or IOs reorient their aid and lending. If industrialized states were the source of the new focus, one would expect to see it first in the arena over which they have most control—bilateral aid. Donor governments would use their bilateral aid packages to press LDCs to reorient their development policies so as to target poor populations more directly. One would also expect to see powerful donor states using their leverage in multilateral institutions to redirect lending toward poverty-related sectors. Again, chronologically, donor states would reorient first.

If the shift toward poverty alleviation were caused by the community of development experts, the expected behavior patterns are less clear. There would have to be a degree of consensus on a clear set of new development principles that elevate poverty as a concern, for without a clear mission and rationale experts are unlikely to influence policy. Furthermore, instead of clear leaders and followers among governments and IOs, one might expect to see relative homogeneity in the shift, for development experts are everywhere. One should nonetheless see the shift occurring more rapidly in those state and IO structures that give access to experts, but there is no reason to think a priori that one or the other should lead the policy move.

If the concern about poverty were promoted by IOs, one would expect to see executive heads and IO staff pushing member states to change their policies rather than the reverse. They would use their resources and expertise to persuade and coerce states into accepting the new anti-poverty policies (i.e., financing them in developed states and adopting them in LDCs). Chronologically, IO development activity would show a poverty orientation before bilateral lending.

25. See Ayres, *Banking on the Poor*, chap. 2 and Meier, *Emerging from Poverty*, chap. 1.

THE INCORPORATION OF POVERTY ALLEVIATION INTO DEVELOPMENT

There are several changes in development activity that, at first glance, appear to be possible sources of the upsurge of interest in poverty alleviation in the 1970s but in fact turn out to have had very limited impact. The creation of the IDA in 1960 was probably the most important of these because it redirected multilateral development activity toward countries where the poor were.[26] In addition to this geographic shift, IDA lending redirected money from industrial, energy, and transport sectors toward agriculture where, as later proponents of poverty alleviation argued, the greatest benefits to the poor could be realized. However, the stated purpose of the IDA's agricultural lending in the 1960s was not poverty alleviation. Indeed, agricultural lending most often went for large investment projects that would benefit large farmers, not poor small farmers (to say nothing of the millions of landless poor in rural areas). Agriculture was important for the IDA principally because it was the most important production sector for the poorest countries, many of which had no significant industrial base in which to invest.[27]

In addition, a few developing countries were also targeting poor populations prior to 1968. India's development plans, from 1961 onward, tried to define and implement a "minimum needs" program—a term that foreshadows the preoccupation with basic human needs after 1970.[28] Socialist countries such as Tanzania and Ghana also articulated distributional concerns in their development plans. In these cases, however, what was changing was conceptions, not simply of development, but of political, social, and economic organization writ large. Poverty alleviation was not the focus of attention; it was only a corollary to larger normative claims being made in these states about legitimate configurations of power—claims that were flatly unacceptable to much of the rest of the international community. Furthermore, despite the egalitarian goals of these states, many of their development strategies still relied heavily on orthodox principles of capital accumulation and public in-

26. Aid consortia and special consultative groups for important borrower countries, such as India and Pakistan, were also set up about this time with similar objectives and effects. See J. H. Adler, "The World Bank's Concept of Development," 42.

27. Ibid. Woods justified a major increase in lending to agriculture (as well as industry) in 1963 on the grounds that it was a "directly productive" sector (as opposed to such "indirectly productive" sectors as utilities). Equity and poverty were not concerns in the shift; nor did this lending target poor populations.

28. This is discussed by John P. Lewis in Lewis and Kallab, eds., *Development Strategies Reconsidered*, 6–7.

vestment. Development projects still were often large-scale enterprises in industrial and transport sectors.[29]

Finally, the Alliance for Progress, launched in 1961, emphasized social programs including poverty. It did not, however, provide a point of departure for global reorientations of development efforts for two reasons. First, the Alliance was aimed primarily at political stabilization, not economic development. The foreign policy agenda of the United States explicitly drove Alliance lending, not concern for the poor. Second, and perhaps related to the first reason, the Alliance was generally considered to be a failure. It was hardly a model likely to prompt emulation elsewhere in the world.[30]

More sustained and globally influential changes occurred in intellectual circles and in the Bank itself. In an intellectual shift, economists began arguing that poverty alleviation should be a primary focus of development efforts in the late 1960s, at roughly the same time that Robert McNamara arrived at the World Bank. Gunnar Myrdal published *Asian Drama: An Inquiry into the Poverty of Nations*, which focused on poverty problems in India and Pakistan, in 1968.[31] That same year, Dudley Seers and a group at the newly founded Institute for Development Studies at the University of Sussex began talking about poverty as part of development.[32] Texts based on these discussions began appearing shortly thereafter.[33] Before that time, the field of development economics had been otherwise occupied. Much of the 1950s and 1960s had been spent on the very basic task of fashioning reasonable models of how LDC economies worked. Development economists recognized that their inherited assumptions about the behavior of factors, price mechanisms, and social institutions were inapplicable to developing countries, but the rejection of these left the new discipline of development economics scrambling for alternatives. The alternatives these economists came up

29. See, for example, Ghana's development plan for 1963–1970. Ghana, Planning Commission, *Seven-year Plan for National Reconstruction and Development.*

30. For more on the Alliance for Progress, see Jerome Levinson and Juan de Onis, *The Alliance That Lost Its Way* (Chicago: Quadrangle Books, 1970).

31. Myrdal continued to push poverty issues onto the agenda with the 1970 publication of *The Challenge of World Poverty*, which probably had a larger impact because of its explicit policy focus. Gunnar Myrdal, *The Challenge of World Poverty: A World Anti-Poverty Program in Outline* (New York: Pantheon Books, 1970).

32. See the discussion in the preface to Dudley Seers and Leonard Joy, *Development in a Divided World* (London: Pelican Books, 1971).

33. For example, Dudley Seers, "The Meaning of Development," *International Development Review* 11 (1969), reprinted and expanded as "What Are We Trying to Measure?" in Nancy Baster, ed., *Measuring Development* (London: Frank Cass, 1972): 21–36.

with initially did not focus on poverty. Arthur Lewis, Raul Prebisch, and the other pioneers of the fifties were preoccupied with industrialization and the lifting of capital constraints; their policies did not target the poor.[34]

The poverty concern among development economists had several sources. The UN and other international secretariats had been collecting data on employment, income distribution, and various aspects of social welfare during the 1960s as part of the "Development Decade." As these were disseminated in the second half of the decade, they made the scope of world poverty startlingly clear. Myrdal suggests that the domestic "unconditional war on poverty" declared by Lyndon Johnson in the United States may also have prompted interest in poverty overseas.[35] The result of the new data and, perhaps, the New Society in the United States was a stinging critique of neo-classical development orthodoxy by many prominent development economists. The problem was not that earlier efforts had failed to do what they had set out to do, i.e., promote growth; the problem was that, despite impressive growth records among LDCs during the 1960s, these policies had "failed" because, the critics argued, they had failed to eliminate poverty. The critique was explicit about its normative element. The aim, as one proponent of the new view wrote in 1971, was to "thrust debates over economic and social development into the arena of ethical values."[36] " 'Development' is inevitably a normative concept," wrote Seers, and massive poverty is "objectionable by any religious or ethical standards."[37] In light of this, the goals of the entire development effort needed to be reassessed.[38]

These attacks on neo-classical orthodoxy were just being launched in the late 1960s and early 1970s; they clearly had not yet triumphed. They were resisted or ignored by development experts in many quarters. That alleviating poverty was desirable was easy to agree upon; that alleviating

34. Growth itself was relatively new as a concern of economics. In *The Theory of Economic Growth* (Homewood, Ill.: R. D. Irwin, 1955), Arthur Lewis commented: "no comprehensive treatise on the subject has been published for about a century. The last great book covering this wide range was John Stuart Mill's *Principles of Political Economy*, published in 1848" (as quoted in Meier, *Emerging from Poverty*, 127). For an extended discussion of the evolution and persistence of static, non-growth models in the field, see Meier, *Emerging from Poverty*, chap. 5.

35. Myrdal, *The Challenge of World Poverty*, xii–xiii.

36. Denis Goulet, *The Cruel Choice: A New Concept in the Theory of Development* (New York: Atheneum, 1971).

37. Seers, "The Meaning of Development," 23.

38. Irma Adelman, "Development Economics: A Reassessment of Goals," *American Economic Review* 65 (1975): 302–309.

poverty was the job of development and development economists was not. How wealth was distributed inside societies was considered a political, not an economic, problem. It involved making explicit value judgments in ways that were supported by neither traditional analytic techniques nor the professional norms of the economics discipline. It made many economists professionally uncomfortable. Instead of creating a clear consensus on new development goals and approprite policies of the type the epistemic community scholars show to be influential, the critics of orthodoxy split the community. What Seers, Joy, Myrdal, and others did by undermining the conventional wisdom was create a permissive environment for change. They drew attention to the failings of previous development policies but did not provide any clear, consensual blueprint for alternative policies. It was in this environment that Robert McNamara assumed the presidency of the World Bank.

A number of changes in Bank policy and organization set the stage for the McNamara agenda when he arrived. When Eugene Black retired as Bank president in 1962, he suggested that the Bank "was approaching the peak of its career and that bankable projects were running out because most potential borrowers had enough debt to carry."[39] The Bank's next president and McNamara's immediate predecessor, George Woods, disagreed. To keep money flowing, he raised the "hemline of bankability" for projects by extending grace periods. Under his leadership, the Bank also began siphoning off funds to support IDA loans (which would benefit the poorest countries), despite earlier promises to the financial community holding Bank bonds that there would be no such mixing of Bank and IDA funds. In an attempt to create more sympathy among Bank staff for LDC projects, Woods sharply increased the proportion of Bank and IDA professional staff who were non-U.S. citizens. He also began to expand the substantive scope of Bank lending, particularly into education and agriculture. Under Woods, lending for tertiary education, particularly technical training, came to be seen as an essential part of LDC industrialization. Similarly, agriculture was recognized as a "directly productive" sector akin to industry, whose stimulation would similarly promote growth.[40] Tertiary technical training obviously did not target

39. "Mr. Woods Looks for New Business," *The Economist* 209 (5 Oct. 1963): 59. See also Michael G. Schechter, "The Political Roles of Recent World Bank Presidents," in Lawrence Finkelstein, ed., *Politics in the United Nations System* (Durham: Duke University Press, 1988), 353; Mason and Asher, *The World Bank*, 458–71.

40. This shift is discussed in both Schechter, "Political Roles," 56–57, and Adler, "The World Bank's Concept of Development," 42–43.

the masses of poor; neither did large loans designed to help "farm business."[41] But these early forays into lending for social and agricultural projects helped create Bank organizational structures for later lending in the name of poverty alleviation.

Robert S. McNamara came to the Bank in 1968 with a background and agenda different from any of his predecessors. He was the first Bank president who was a manager, not a banker.[42] He had been an assistant professor at Harvard Business School before joining Ford Motor Company, which named him president in 1960. From 1961 to 1968, he served as secretary of defense under Presidents Kennedy and Johnson. As contemporary and later commentators observed, he was a "classic Kennedy activist" who believed "very obviously in the 'exercise of power' " and brought to the Bank a clear set of goals toward which that power was to be directed.[43] Those goals centered around a deeply-held belief in the virtues and efficacy of foreign aid. McNamara believed that aid was a moral obligation of rich nations and that it could and did work. He was an internationalist driven by internationalist morality and optimism. By helping the poor, rich nations could answer the moral imperative and serve their own interests at the same time. Because poverty caused violence, internationally as well as domestically, rich nations could create a more stable and secure world for themselves by alleviating the poverty of others.[44] McNamara had expressed these views well before he arrived at the Bank.

41. "Mr. Woods Looks for New Business," 59. According to one Bank staffer, "until the arrival of Robert McNamara, lending for agriculture remained of the traditional type, predominantly plantation or commercial agriculture, largely influenced by the experience of former colonial agricultural officers who constituted a large proportion of the Bank's agricultural staff. By the time I came to the Bank's Western Africa Regional Office in 1968, the Bank had financed only one agricultural project in the 24 countries of the region." Roger Chaufournier, "The Coming of Age," *Finance and Development* 21 (June 1984): 34.

42. McNamara made it very clear that he regarded the Bank primarily as a development agency rather than a bank. He is quoted as saying, "If I had wanted to run a bank, I would have been a banker" in Schechter, "Political Roles," 363.

43. Ibid., and "Robert McNamara, Banker" *The Economist* 227 (8 Jun. 1968): 70–71. For McNamara's own account of his views on development and his plans for the Bank see Robert S. McNamara, *One Hundred Countries, Two Billion People* (New York: Praeger, 1973).

44. There is a thesis that McNamara's antipoverty crusade at the World Bank was a form of expiation for his "sins" in Vietnam. See, for example, Henry Trewhitt, "Power on the Potomac: The Agony and the Expiation of Robert McNamara," *Washingtonian* 7 (November 1971): 35–38. This thesis does not explain, however, the earlier articulations of concern about poverty in McNamara's pre-Bank days, before the commission and recognition of his "sins." The precise origin of McNamara's antipoverty commitment would require a psychobiography that reaches beyond the scope of this chapter. Deborah Shapley, in her recent biography, treats this subject only briefly but does identify as one important source a group of British development thinkers, principally William Clark and Barbara Ward.

In a speech to the American Society of Newspaper Editors in Montreal in 1966, while still secretary of defense, McNamara argued the importance of ending poverty in the developing world for both humanitarian and security reasons, emphasizing the limitations of military power to achieve security goals in a world with such gross disparities of welfare.[45]

McNamara's attack on world poverty came on two fronts. The first of these was Bank lending, which doubled in volume in his first five years in office. McNamara was concerned that, after the initial enthusiasm of the early 1960s, developed countries were becoming disillusioned with foreign aid. He cited a "mood of frustration and failure" surrounding the efforts of the Development Decade and feared that developed countries would begin to reduce aid as a result. His response was to use both the Bank's financial resources and his political position to insure and increase aid flows to poor countries.[46] His concerns about bilateral giving were well founded. While Official Development Assistance (ODA) from the OECD's Development Assistance Committee (DAC) grew steadily in constant dollars until about 1965, DAC giving from 1965 through 1972 remained flat. See Table 1. Indeed, as a percentage of GNP, ODA for DAC countries declined steadily during the 1960s. See Table 2.[47]

McNamara was "spellbound" by Ward when he first heard her speak during his Kennedy cabinet years. "She influenced me more than anyone in my life," McNamara said later. Clark was already at the Bank when McNamara arrived, and the two hit it off. He was extremely well connected in the Fabian-inspired British development circles concerned with poverty issues (of which Ward was also part) and made sure that McNamara met and heard from these critics of development orthodoxy. Deborah Shapley, *Promise and Power: The Life and Times of Robert S. McNamara* (Boston: Little, Brown, 1993), 503–12, quotations on 506 and 507.

45. Shapley, *Promise and Power*, 381–82. "Everything we have done in Vietnam won't count for a thing if Indian democracy goes down the drain," McNamara remarked to Chester Bowles, U.S. ambassador to India, during the battle to secure additional IDA funding for that country in the early months of McNamara's tenure at the Bank. Shapley, *Power and Promise*, 465. *The Economist*'s profile of McNamara in June 1968 also mentions his long-term attention to foreign aid during his seven years at the Pentagon and criticizes his concern for the poorest countries, least able to repay loans, rather than "those countries who already happen to have a good chance of lifting themselves out of the mire," to which *The Economist* would have preferred to see loans made. "Robert McNamara, Banker," 71

46. John Maddux discusses this in some detail in *The Development Philosophy of Robert S. McNamara* (Washington, D.C.: World Bank, 1981). McNamara himself was clear about this strategy in his speeches and writings. McNamara, *The McNamara Years at the World Bank: Major Policy Addresses of Robert S. McNamara, 1968–1981* (Baltimore: The Johns Hopkins University Press for the World Bank, 1981) and McNamara, *One Hundred Countries*, 7–12.

47. For more on bilateral aid trends see OECD, *Development Cooperation: 1975 Review*, 154; Meier, *Emerging from Poverty*, 46. Note that aggregate DAC data disguise variations among donor states. U.S. aid, which is by far the largest component of DAC giving, dropped sharply, from 0.46 percent of GNP in 1965–1969 to 0.28 percent in 1970–1974.

Table 1. Trends in ODA volume from DAC countries (four-year moving averages at 1983 prices and exchange rates), in billions $U.S.

1963–1966	1965–1968	1967–1970	1969–1972	1971–1974	1973–1976	1975–1978
18.6	18.9	18.5	18.6	18.9	19.4	21.3

SOURCE: OECD, *Twenty-five Years of Development Cooperation: A Review* (Paris: OECD, 1985), 95.

Table 2. Trends in ODA/GNP of DAC members

1965	1966	1967	1968	1969	1970	1971	1972	1973	1974	1975
0.48	0.43	0.41	0.41	0.36	0.33	0.33	0.35	0.29	0.33	0.35

SOURCE: OECD, *Twenty-five Years of Development Cooperation: A Review* (Paris: OECD, 1985), 97, and World Bank, *IDA in Retrospect* (New York: Oxford University Press, 1982), 14.

In addition to increasing the quantity of aid, McNamara wanted to change the way in which aid was used. As a self-perceived manager of a development agency rather than a commercial banker, McNamara took a much more active interest in what LDC states actually did with the money they received from the Bank and in the kinds of effects (if any) the aid was having. McNamara was the first president of the Bank to order routine evaluations of Bank activities and to create a standing branch of the organization for this purpose. He loved charts and figures and was strongly struck by the new data, mentioned above, revealing the extent of world poverty.

From his first speech to the Board of Governors in his second month in office, McNamara put poverty issues on the table. He spoke not only of GNP per capita but of directing Bank lending toward improving the living conditions of individual poor people. He proposed expanding education lending to *all* levels of education, emphasizing fundamental literacy as well as more advanced technical training. He spoke of basic nutritional requirements for individual health and well-being and of lending for the benefits of individual peasant farmers as well as farming business.[48] A month later, in a speech to the Inter-American Press Association, McNamara made "economic and social policies which will permit a more equitable distribution" of wealth the first of his demands from borrowing countries.[49] Unlike his predecessors, he talked about "the poor" as individual human beings rather than as countries, and emphasized poorer segments within societies rather than simply classifying entire countries as poor.[50] Thus, from the time he arrived in 1968, McNamara understood his central mission to be doing something about world poverty. The questions were "what" and "how." Between 1968 and 1973, when he outlined a comprehensive program in Nairobi, McNa-

---

Giving by other large states—the United Kingdom, West Germany, Japan, and France—also dropped in this period, albeit much less sharply. However, giving by smaller states—Canada, Denmark, Finland, the Netherlands, New Zealand, Norway, and Sweden—rose in this period and among the Scandanavian countries giving rose sharply. This variation would be in keeping with the hypothesis about international consequences of domestic social welfare politics in Scandanavian states advanced by Lumsdaine in *Moral Vision* and discussed below. For data, see Lumsdaine, *Moral Vision*, table 4.6, p. 133.

48. Speech to the Board of Governors of the World Bank, Washington D.C., 30 September 1968. Reprinted in McNamara, *The McNamara Years*, 3–15.

49. Speech to the Inter-American Press Association, Buenos Aries, 18 October 1968. Reprinted in McNamara, *The McNamara Years*, 25.

50. Escott Reid, "McNamara's World Bank," *Foreign Affairs* 51 (1973): 794–810, especially 794.

mara struggled with these problems of securing both the means and the strategy for attacking poverty.

To make a dent in a problem as massive as world poverty, McNamara clearly needed a bigger and somewhat different Bank.[51] In his first speech to the Board of Governors, he therefore proposed doubling Bank lending in his first five years.[52] This meant that the Bank would lend nearly as much in the 1969–1973 period as it had in its entire 22-year history.[53] Doing this obligated McNamara to borrow more and borrow at rates above its current lending rate, policies that made many in Western governments and financial circles uncomfortable and were opposed by more than half of McNamara's senior Bank staff.[54]

Simply having more money did not ensure that more money was going to the poor, however. To tackle this problem, McNamara reconfigured the financial relationship between the Bank and the IDA, whose responsibility it was to serve the poorest countries. Given a global recession and donor states' lack of enthusiasm for aid (especially the United States), securing large replenishments for the IDA proved difficult. McNamara's response was to begin funneling IBRD surplus funds to the IDA. Again, senior staff and world financial figures were unhappy and predicted dire consequences for confidence in the Bank's operations and the Bank's ability to raise funds on world markets (fears which appear not to have been borne out). Furthermore, he endorsed proposals to provide the IDA with $3 billion per year in special drawing rights (SDRs) from the IMF.[55]

In addition to expanding the size of the Bank, McNamara also had to change its organizational structure and style. Before his arrival, the Bank had operated with a style termed by one high-level staffer "leisurely perfectionism." Staff followed projects in minute detail and took months to make decisions.[56] Doubling the volume and changing the direction of

51. Thinking big was clearly McNamara's style. During his Defense Department days, McNamara became accustomed to having large institutional resources at his disposal with which he could have large effects on the world stage. The relatively small size of the Bank was something new to him. "At first he kept talking in billions and then he would correct himself and say 'I meant millions,' " recalls one Bank staffer, William Clark quoted in Shapley, *Power and Promise*, 471.

52. Speech to the Board of Governors of the World Bank, Washington D.C., 30 September 1968. Reprinted in McNamara, *The McNamara Years*, 3–15.

53. Schechter, "Political Roles," 362.

54. "Robert McNamara, Banker;" Ayres, *Banking on the Poor*, 61–64.

55. Reid, "McNamara's World Bank," 805.

56. The old style also clashed with McNamara's own. It left the Bank underutilized and was, in McNamara's words, "an inefficient way to run a planet." William Clark, quoted in Shapley, *Power and Promise*, 477.

lending quickly made this style unworkable. Both changes required more staff, more work, and less attention to detail.[57] The "new style" of poverty-oriented lending (described below) entailed lending for more small projects based on less information, using less well-developed techniques, and involving more costs and benefits that were difficult or impossible to quantify using standard economic analytic tools. The results were predictable: resistance among staff to new methods and policies, conflicts between old and new staff, conflicts among project and program staff, and uncertainty among both staff and borrowers.[58]

McNamara's response to these demands on his institution was to turn what had been a club into a bureaucracy. The Bank was always a very "presidential" institution. McNamara used those extensive presidential powers and expanded them. He turned the Bank into a much more hierarchical place, gathering to himself the reins of power and streamlining the organization. His consolidation of power extended even to his relationship with the executive directors, the representatives of the member countries who must approve Bank actions.[59]

At the same time that McNamara was building this expanded instrument for attacking poverty, he was also thinking about strategies for the attack. Studies coming out in 1968–1969, including the Pearson Report initiated by the Bank, made it abundantly clear that the benefits of growth were not "trickling down" to the poorest.[60] There was, however, little consensus on an alternative policy that would improve the lot of poor populations. Defining and articulating this policy alternative became a preoccupation of McNamara's initial years in office. In true Whiz Kid style, McNamara sought out new ideas and solutions and brought

57. In fact, doing both simultaneously proved difficult. Escott Reid, a former Bank employee, describes the frustration of Bank officers. They could meet the volume goals more easily by processing old-style infrastructure loans for dams and roads, which were big-ticket projects requiring relatively little oversight. Alternatively, they could explore new kinds of lending projects that targeted poor populations, but these projects tended to move less money and require more supervision. Reid, "McNamara's World Bank," 796.

58. William Ascher gives an excellent discussion of the organizational impact of the antipoverty orientation on the Bank in "New Development Approaches and the Adaptability of International Agencies: The Case of the World Bank," *International Organization* 37 (1983): 415–39. Jonathan Sanford also discusses some of these issues, and Robert Ayres discusses at length the organizational dimensions of implementing poverty policies. See Johnathan Sanford, "The World Bank and Poverty: A Review of the Evidence on Whether the Agency has Diminished Emphasis on Aid to the Poor," *American Journal of Economics and Sociology* 48 (1989): 151–64, especially 159; and Ayres, *Banking on the Poor.*

59. Schechter, "Political Roles"; Ayres, *Banking on the Poor,* 64–67; Shapley, *Power and Promise,* 479–80.

60. Harry G. Johnson, "Pearson's 'Grand Assize' Fails," *Round Table* 237 (1970): 17–25.

people articulating these ideas into the Bank's orbit. They were not lawyers and bankers, for the most part, but economists and managers.[61] Hollis Chenery, for example, was a Harvard economist who put the Bank on the cutting edge of research in development economics and made essential connections with Dudley Seers and the Sussex crowd. Their collaborative book, *Redistribution with Growth*, a joint effort between Bank staff and academics, redefined intellectual thinking in the field.[62] Mahbub ul Haq, who became head of Policy, Planning, and Program Review at the Bank, was a former finance minister of Pakistan. Having been a strong advocate of growth strategies earlier, in the late 1960s and early 1970s he became a passionate advocate for rethinking development to solve poverty problems.[63] In addition to hiring new full-time senior staff, McNamara commissioned reports, brought in people to give seminars or work on short consultancy contracts with in-house task forces he set up. For example, McNamara met Alan Berg, an expert on nutrition issues, at a Brookings Institution seminar and was sufficiently interested in his ideas to bring him in to the Bank for a time.[64]

Between 1968 and 1970 many different kinds of poverty-alleviation policies were proposed at the Bank. Population control was an early focus of attention: if only something could be done to control the population explosion in these developing countries, there would be more wealth to go around. Nutrition projects were suggested as a focus of Bank activity: many of the world's poor were so malnourished that they could not do productive work and raise themselves out of poverty. Health projects were proposed under much the same rationale. Education was explored in great detail as a means of increasing labor productivity. Labor-intensive industries were discussed as a means of alleviating unemployment.

The particular set of policies the Bank settled on in 1970–1971 had less to do with any intrinsic merit of one policy over another than with

61. Shapley recounts the story of McNamara's recruitment of former Securities and Exchange Commission lawyer Eugene Rotberg. During the interview McNamara ascertained that Rotberg knew nothing about international finance, that his education was in English literature, history, and law, and that he thought most investment bankers should be jailed under the Sherman Antitrust Act. Learning this, McNamara asked him if he would accept the post of treasurer of the World Bank. Rotberg did. Shapley, *Power and Promise*, 471–72.

62. Hollis Chenery, *Redistribution with Growth: Policies to Improve Income Distribution in Developing Countries in the Context of Economic Growth: A Joint Study [Commissioned] by the World Bank's Development Research Center and the Institute of Development Studies, University of Sussex* (London: Oxford University Press for the World Bank and the Institute of Development Studies, 1974).

63. Haq, *Poverty Curtain;* Shapley, *Power and Promise*, 508–9.

64. Richard Webb, World Bank History Project, personal communication, 9 June 1993.

which policy would best answer the organizational requirements and fit the organizational competencies of the Bank. Population control was McNamara's early personal favorite. In his early months in office, he made several high-profile speeches in which he made it clear that he believed population was the overriding cause of poverty in the developing world.[65] The demographic characteristics of these policies were easily quantifiable and so appeared congenial to him. But population control did not match the organizational requirements of the Bank. First, it was too political. It inserted the Bank into a debate that was fundamentally about values and religion in a way that Bank staffers, as well many outside the Bank, found objectionable. As William Ascher's study makes clear, the professional norms of bank staffers were enormously important in determining their reaction to policy changes. Most of the Bank staff were economists by training and understood their roles as technical or managerial. They prided themselves on being able to provide rigorous analyses of development problems, and many became profoundly uncomfortable when asked to make what they perceived to be value judgements without sound technical guidelines and methods.[66] Furthermore, while population control represented a new poverty-oriented direction for lending, it did not help the Bank meet its other goal of doubling the volume of lending. Population projects simply did not absorb a lot of money—certainly not in comparison with power plants and dams—and moving money was a major preoccupation of the Bank during McNamara's first five years. Finally, the Bank lacked expertise, experience, and therefore credibility in the field of population control. This not only made staffers uncomfortable, it made borrowers suspicious. The Bank plays an active role in the design and supervision of projects it funds, so entering the politically sensitive area of population control was unattractive enough to borrower governments; doing so as the Bank's guinea pigs was even less attractive.

Proposals that the Bank begin major forays into the areas of health and nutrition also made little headway. In part, this was a result of the Bank's lack of expertise and credibility in these areas; in part it was because these areas were understood to be the specialization of other in-

65. Most notable was his speech to the largely Catholic audience at the University of Notre Dame, Notre Dame, Indiana, 1 May 1969, reprinted in McNamara, *The McNamara Years*, 33–52. McNamara's personal interest in population control continued even after it was sidelined by the Bank as is evident from the subject's prominence in his writings. See, for example, McNamara, *One Hundred Countries*, passim.

66. Ascher, "New Development Approaches," 429–35; Ayres, *Banking on the Poor*, 38–41.

ternational organizations, such as the FAO and WHO.[67] Education fared somewhat better. The Bank had already established a track record there under George Woods. What was needed was a shift toward lending for mass literacy campaigns to supplement the narrower lending for tertiary technical training that the Bank was already funding. However, the relationship between literacy and alleviating poverty was somewhat indirect. Teaching people to read did not, by itself, feed or shelter people. A more direct strategy was needed.

The policy that the Bank finally hit upon was rural development and aid to small subsistence farmers. The Bank estimated that between 550 and 700 million people were living in rural poverty, most in some kind of subsistence or sub-subsistence farming situations. The technology of the Green Revolution, then becoming widely known, could be used to help these very large poor populations. What was needed was an integrated, multi-sector approach toward developing an entire impoverished region. By simultaneously providing agricultural credits, limited irrigation, roads to markets, improved seed stock, education, and training in new cultivation techniques in ways that would be mutually reinforcing, entire areas could be lifted out of poverty.[68] The organizational attractions of this approach were many. First, the Bank had experience lending in agriculture, even if not to small farmers. Second, these regional projects could absorb a lot of money (thus satisfying the volume goals) and channel it directly toward the world's poorest populations. Third, many, if not all, of the aspects of these rural regional development projects could be addressed with professional skills possessed by the Bank staff—certainly more so than with the population projects. Finally, these projects were attractive to borrower governments. While LDCs had not shown any particular interest in channeling Bank funds directly toward the poor, these multi-sector projects did have the advantage of offering something for a variety of different governmental ministries in borrower states—agriculture for the agriculture ministries, roads for the transport ministry, training for the education ministry.[69]

67. Interview, Richard Webb, World Bank History Project, June 1993. Population, health, and nutrition projects were ultimately funded as part of the overall antipoverty effort but they never absorbed more than 1 percent of the Bank's total lending. Michael Lipton and Alexander Shakow, "The World Bank and Poverty," *Finance and Development* 19 (1982): 16–19; Ayres, *Banking on the Poor*, 6.

68. Ayres, *Banking on the Poor*, chap. 5; A. M. J. van de Laar, *The World Bank and the World's Poor* (Institute for Social Studies, Occasional Paper Series, no. 58, 1976).

69. Webb interview.

This set of policies did not emerge overnight. While the poverty focus was present from the beginning of McNamara's tenure at the Bank, the focused rural development program did not appear until 1970 and 1971. It was not institutionalized until 1972, when the Bank set up a specialized unit for rural development, and did not arrive on center stage of the world development community's debates until McNamara outlined it in his famous 1973 Nairobi speech.[70]

From the Nairobi speech onward, the momentum behind the antipoverty program snowballed. Having achieved his goal of doubling funds since 1968, McNamara was able to shift that money very quickly into rural development projects. He had created a new branch of the Bank a year earlier to deal directly with rural development, and trends in lending shifted quickly away from the old industrial sectors and toward agriculture and rural development. The share of agriculture increased from 12 percent of total Bank lending in the period 1961–1965 to 16 percent in 1971–1972 and 24 percent in 1973–1974.[71] Rural development lending increased from 2.9 percent of total IBRD/IDA lending in 1969 to 4.9 percent in 1972, 7.5 percent in 1973 and 11 percent in 1974.[72] As these percentages rose, the share of Bank lending going to infrastructure projects (power plants, dams, and roads) fell. In 1967, such projects consumed 55 percent of bank lending; by 1977, they consumed 30 percent.[73] In addition to this sectoral shift the Bank increased the share of its loans to the poorest countries. Of its agricultural lending, the Bank had allocated 22.5 percent of its loans to its poorest class of countries (those with GNP per capita of less than $150) and 49.3 percent of its loans to countries with GNP per capita above $376 during the period 1964–1968. In 1969–1974 that poorest class of countries received 38.2 percent of loans, while those above $376 per capita received only 31.7 percent.[74]

70. McNamara speech to the Board of Governors, Nairobi, Kenya, 24 September 1973, reprinted in McNamara, *The McNamara Years*, 233–63.

71. World Bank, *The Assault on World Poverty* (Baltimore: The Johns Hopkins University Press, 1975) 11, 58. In absolute terms, the increase is even more striking. In fiscal years 1969 through 1971, the Bank and IDA loaned as much for agriculture as they had in the previous two decades. See Mason and Asher, *The World Bank*, 204.

72. World Bank, *The Assault on World Poverty*, 88.

73. Mahbub ul Haq, "Changing Emphasis of the Bank's Lending Policies," *Finance and Development* 15 (1978): 13.

74. World Bank, *The Assault on World Poverty*, 85. These World Bank tables do not specify the year for which GNP per capita was calculated or what was done to control for inflation as countries migrated out of GNP per capita categories over time, not due to increasing wealth but due to inflation. The DAC data used below are similarly unclear. In both cases, percentage of Bank lending or DAC ODA flows to countries with GNP per

Robert Ayres provides an excellent overview of the expansion and evolution of the Bank's antipoverty activities. The most important additions to the Bank's program were the urban poverty projects to provide "sites and services," such as potable water, food, and medical care to the urban poor—as opposed to building large structures such as apartment buildings, which inevitably ended up costing more than the poorest could afford.[75] These projects shared the organizational advantages of the rural development projects: ability to absorb lots of money and a multi-sector character that created wide appeal in borrower government bureaucracies. Ayres also provides extensive documentation of the Bank's efforts to promote its notions about poverty among its borrower states. He describes the implementation of rural development projects despite resistance from large, entrenched agricultural interests in Nigeria, land tenure problems in Latin America, and weak national institutions in Tanzania, Haiti, and Paraguay. In some cases, the Bank's methods of implementation were coercive, as in the Mexican Papaloapan River Basin Project, in which the Bank simply withheld funds from Mexican officials who wanted a dam instead of a rural development project in the region.[76] More often, the Bank seems to have used methods of persuasion and co-optation. The use of locals rather than expatriates to staff projects, as in West Africa and Bolivia, created new groups within LDCs who were actively committed to the Bank's antipoverty goals and programs. More important, the poor beneficiaries of Bank projects often mobilized and organized as a result of their contact with the Bank and its ideas, pressing for further antipoverty measures. Ayres documents cases of this in Haiti, Bolivia, the Philippines, and Tanzania.[77]

The Bank's activities also influenced the shift in intellectual development circles toward a poverty orientation. As was mentioned earlier, the growth-oriented intellectual orthodoxy was under attack in 1968 from poverty-focused critics such as Seers and Myrdal. The Bank's switch in approach did much to legitimize the critics and institutionalize the new wisdom as essential to development. The Bank's research

---

capita under $150 in 1969 prices might be given one year; percentage of DAC ODA flows to countries with GNP per capita under $199 in 1976 prices are given another year. This recurring problem makes it difficult to comparing lending by recipient income group over time. In this case, however, if countries are migrating out of the group with GNP per capita under $150 due to inflation, the shift in Bank lending is all the more impressive.

75. Lipton and Shakow, "The World Bank and Poverty"; Edward Jaycox, "The Bank and Urban Poverty," *Finance and Development* 15 (1978): 10–13.

76. Ayres, *Banking on the Poor*, 116.

77. Ibid., 139–40.

work was widely respected even before McNamara's arrival. With his gravitational pull of academic talent into the Bank, its reputation and influence increased further and was brought to bear on the problem of providing intellectual support for the anti-poverty effort. Bank policy papers, which began circulating in the early 1970s, drew large audiences and influenced thinking in both national and international development agencies.[78] Chenery's collaboration with the academic community of development scholars at Sussex to produce *Redistribution with Growth* was a landmark in reorienting thinking in both the academic and international policy communities toward poverty-focused development.

Poverty concerns, once established as part of the development mission, remained firmly fixed. The whole effort might have been stillborn, however, for within weeks of the Nairobi speech, OPEC members quadrupled the price of oil, sending the industrialized world into a panic and making it harder for McNamara to put the poor high on the agendas of rich nations. He was able to counter this blow and save his Nairobi program by turning to OPEC states as a source for the Bank's commercial borrowing.[79] Anti-poverty concerns continued to survive and even expand despite the second oil shocks and global recession of the late seventies and early eighties. While the international economic community, including the Bank, retrenched during this period and began promoting "structural adjustment" in LDCs, it did so with an eye to the effects on the poor. It even justified these policies at times as the best way, in the long run, to help the world's poor.[80] The Bank continually conducted studies of the effects of structural adjustment policies on the poor, and debate raged, both inside the Bank and outside, about the effects these policies were having on the poor.

During the late 1970s and early 1980s, the Bank continued to shift its lending toward the poorest countries. In 1975, 29 percent of total IBRD/IDA lending was going to the poorest countries (in this case, those with annual per capita incomes below $420 in 1985 dollars). While this figure fell slightly during the late 1970s, it rose steadily during the 1980s—the heyday of structural adjustment. See Table 3.

---

78. Many of the early poverty policy papers are collected in World Bank, *Assault on World Poverty*.

79. McNamara's attempts to obtain OPEC funding on concessional terms failed. Shapley, *Promise and Power*, 516–19.

80. See, for example, A. W. Clausen, "Absolute Poverty Can Be Eliminated," *Pakistan and Gulf Economist* 4 (16 Feb. 1985): 45–46.

Table 3. Shares of World Bank lending going to the world's poorest countries (percentages)

	1975	1976	1977	1978	1979	1980	1981	1982	1983	1984	1985	1986	1987
IBRD/IDA	29	27	24	25	26	26	28	31	33	38	40	36	38
IDA only	83	89	85	80	77	77	87	90	88	89	94	89	94

Source: Jonathan Sanford, "The World Bank and Poverty: A Review of the Evidence on Whether the Agency Has Diminished Emphasis on Aid to the Poor." *American Journal of Economics and Sociology* 48, 2 (April 1989): 152.

Whether and how structural adjustment policies actually affected poverty are important questions; however, they are not the questions I am addressing in this study. What is important here is that poverty alleviation continued to be central to all debates about development policy. Attempts to refocus development on growth issues now had to address and compete with champions of distributional concerns. The continued shift in lending and the vigor of the debate over poverty show how deeply entrenched poverty alleviation had become as part of the development mission.[81]

The Bank's role as the driving force behind poverty concerns becomes even clearer when we examine the behavior of states in this period. Developing states, for the most part, were receptive to the Bank's new antipoverty focus, but they were not activists or initiators. Even in its old-style lending, the Bank has never worked the way a commercial bank does—waiting for borrowers to approach it with possible projects to fund. Instead, the Bank has always been heavily involved in what it calls "project identification." It goes out and identifies projects which it believes might be "fundable" and helps borrowers develop those project proposals to insure that the loan can, in fact, be granted. This project identification role was intensified with the new antipoverty focus. Having decided that poverty alleviation was to be an important goal, someone had to come up with strategies for doing this. Those someones were Bank staffers. It was not the case that LDC governments put forward antipoverty proposals of their own which were judged by the Bank (although LDCs did review and object to some of the Bank's proposals; for example, those concerning population control). Instead it fell to the Bank to come up with strategies for achieving the new goals it had proposed. The Bank staff, not the borrowers, had to go out and look for new poverty projects, design those projects, and then "sell" them to LDC governments. The most popular type of project was the rural development project discussed above.

The lack of LDC initiative and enthusiasm for antipoverty projects has three explanations. First, the domestic political structures of many of these governments were such that elites in power actually had much more to gain politically and materially from the conventional large in-

81. For a detailed discussion of the Bank's balancing of poverty concerns with structural adjustment policies, see Jonathan Sanford, "The World Bank and Poverty: the Plight of the World's Impoverished Is Still a Major Concern of the International Agency," *American Journal of Economics and Sociology* 47 (1988): 257–75. Sanford supplies extensive data showing that the Bank policies have continued to reflect an antipoverty orientation.

frastructure projects, in which power and money remained in the hands of elites, than in projects directed toward the rural poor, from which domestic elites often could reap fewer political or material benefits.[82] Second, the poor were not politically important in most of these countries; thus, there was little incentive for LDC governments to direct precious resources toward them. Third, LDCs during this period were pushing an alternative and much more sweeping "antipoverty" strategy—the New International Economic Order (NIEO). The solution to poverty implicit and often explicit in the NIEO was not directing investment toward poor populations but restructuring the international economy. Projects such as the Bank's could treat only the symptoms of global poverty, in this view; a cure required something much more drastic.[83] Thus, LDCs accepted these antipoverty projects more as the price of continued funding for other, more desired projects and as the price for the continued good will of the Bank than out of concern about poverty.

Although LDCs did little to initiate poverty alleviation as a central concern, they subsequently endorsed it in international forums[84] and quickly adopted it in their own development plans and policies.[85] They accepted and accommodated the World Bank's antipoverty projects. Furthermore, they systematically began incorporating antipoverty goals as central parts of their national development plans. A perusal of the national development plans of several of the most important and most populous LDCs during the 1960s and 1970s shows a systematic change in statements of development aims and objectives in all these plans in the mid-1970s, immediately following the World Bank's change in emphasis.

Indonesia's first five year plan (1969–1974), for example, outlined a very conventional, growth-oriented plan emphasizing government activ-

---

82. Reid, "McNamara's World Bank," 802.

83. For more on the NIEO, see Craig Murphy, "What the Third World Wants: An Interpretation of the Development and Meaning of the New International Economic Order Ideology," *International Studies Quarterly* 27 (1983): 55–76. Note, too, that despite some of its rhetoric the NIEO was more interested in LDC power than poverty. See Stephen D. Krasner, *Structural Conflict: The Third World against Global Liberalism* (Berkeley: University of California Press, 1985).

84. For example, the non-aligned countries meeting in Colombo, Sri Lanka, in August 1976, called for the "eradication of unemployment and poverty" through the implementation of "basic human needs" policies. International Labour Office, *Employment, Growth, and Basic Needs: A One-World Problem* (New York: Praeger, 1977), viii.

85. It must be reiterated that I make no claims about the *effectiveness* of these plans or policies, nor do I presume to judge the sincerity of LDC governments in their policies and pronouncements about poverty. My concern is with changes in the collectively held norms about the development effort, not with realization of those normative goals.

ity in infrastructure construction, industry, agriculture (not small farmers but "estate agriculture"), mining, petroleum development, and the like. There is only one sentence about social welfare (on p.62) and no mention of poverty alleviation or problems of income distribution.[86] The second five year plan, however (1974–1975 to 1978–1979), reflects the shift in development thinking:

> In translating the overriding goals into concrete programs and policies, the Plan provides guidelines for the creation of expanding employment opportunities, a rising level of income, a more equitable distribution of income, a more even distribution of the gains of development among the various regions of the country. . . . The specific objectives of the Second Plan are provision of sufficient and better food and clothing, the provision of housing materials and other facilities to the general public, the improvement and expansion of the infrastructure, the expansion and more equitable distribution of social welfare facilities, and the creation of greater employment opportunities.[87]

In Nigeria, the 1962–1968 plan's "principal feature . . . is its gearing for growth." It says nothing about poverty, equity, social justice, or income distribution in its statement of objectives.[88] By 1975, the 1975–1980 Plan's primary objective is "to achieve a rapid increase in the standard of living." This Plan states explicitly on the first page:

> development is not just a matter of growth in per capita income. It is possible to record a high growth rate in per capita income while the masses of the people continue to be in abject poverty and lacking in the basic necessities of life. . . . An important objective of the plan, therefore, is to spread the benefits of economic development so that the average Nigerian would experience a marked improvement in his standard of living.[89]

Conclusive evidence about the cause of this change would require a detailed investigation into the policymaking processes of these countries; however, the synchronous nature of the change, its timing, and the fact that these development plans were all submitted to the Bank as part of

86. Indonesia, Department of Information, *Development.*
87. Indonesia, Department of Information, *Indonesia Develops: Repelita II, Second Five Year Development Plan, 1974/75–1978/79* (Djakarta, 1974).
88. Nigeria, *Federal Government Development Programme.*
89. Nigeria, Federal Ministry of Economic Development, *Third National Development Plan, 1975–80* (Lagos: Federal Printing Office, 1975).

loan applications strongly suggest that the Bank's new agenda sparked the shift in state plans.[90]

Developed states, too, were receptive to the new approach but did not initiate it. As indicated above, foreign aid was on the decline among the developed countries during the early McNamara years when the Bank was beginning to articulate its new set of poverty concerns. McNamara's objective on coming into office—to double Bank lending in his first five years—was greeted with some skepticism, not only by many of the Bank's senior staff, but also by government officials in many developed countries from which the Bank raised funds. Certainly, developed states were not pushing McNamara either to step up Bank activity or to redirect its efforts toward the poor.

If developed states were not using their power in the Bank to shift its direction, there remains the possibility that the poverty focus in the development community originated not at the Bank, but in the national aid strategies of developed states. The Bank may simply have copied the poverty focus from bilateral aid policies of member states. This proposition appears unlikely for two reasons. First, there is no evidence to support it. World Bank documents and reports do not cite bilateral aid policies as models, do not involve experts from particular states in describing donor state policies, and do not cite policy debates or government reports in donor states that promote this kind of poverty focus. Rather, the Bank discussions reflect a strong sense of being in uncharted territory and at times being at a loss for policy options to meet these new poverty goals. Furthermore, the annual OECD reports on DAC aid do not begin to emphasize poverty alleviation until December 1972, at which time the discussion is entirely about recommendations for future member actions; nothing is said and no data are supplied about actual DAC member policy reorientation or changed patterns of giving that might suggest that poverty-oriented policies were already in place or even being contemplated in member states. In addition, Bank lending shifts toward poverty-oriented sectors such as agriculture and social services occur before aggregate DAC ODA does. As shown in Table 4, Bank lending was already shifting toward poverty-oriented projects and poor populations before 1973.

90. Other development plans and policies surveyed include those of Ghana, Honduras, India, Jordan, Malaysia, Thailand, and Turkey. Thailand is the one outlier in this group. Its development plans begin to talk about increasing welfare, the standard of living, and even rural development as early as 1967.

Bank lending for "directly poverty oriented sectors" tripled between the 1968–1970 period and 1971–1973. Similarly, lending to low-income countries (below $680 GNP per capita in 1979 dollars) increased 6 percentage points, or roughly 16 percent, above the previous level between the pre-1968 and the 1969–1973 periods.[91] DAC did not keep analogous poverty-oriented data during this period (itself suggestive of the absence of a poverty orientation.)[92] However, the picture that emerges from the data available is not one of leadership in retargeting the development effort. The clearest aid preoccupations in the 1968–1973 period were, first, to keep the volume of ODA from DAC countries from declining any further and, second, to improve the conditions of DAC aid; i.e., increase the percentage of grants, as opposed to loans; improve the terms of loans; and increase the percentage of "untied" aid.[93]

Other possible indicators of a shift toward poverty-focused aid do not show much change until after 1975, when the Bank's efforts are already well under way. Changes in the sectoral distribution of development assistance were widely understood to be a necessary part of targeting the poor, not only in the Bank but in the development community generally, including the DAC.[94] As donor states are persuaded to incorporate poverty-focused policies, we might expect to see sectoral shifts in giving turn away from industry, energy, and transport, and toward agriculture. While the data are sketchy, these shifts do not appear to occur during this period. Capital project assistance for agriculture projects (as a percentage of total bilateral ODA) remains relatively flat: 2.41 percent in 1967–1968, 3.6 percent in 1971, 2.3 percent in 1972.[95] Even in the 1973–1975 period, increases in funding for agriculture as a percentage of all DAC ODA are not clear or consistent. See Table 5. It does appear, however, that the appeals to shift lending toward agriculture eventually,

91. World Bank, *Focus on Poverty: A Report of a Task Force of the World Bank*, Joint Bank-Fund Library, Washington, D.C., Photocopy, 1982.

92. In fact, DAC data on purposes and sectoral allocations of aid are maddeningly inconsistent across the various issues of the annual report. Data collected in one year are often not collected again, making sectoral change over time difficult to measure.

93. See the review of 1965–1975 period in OECD, *Development Cooperation: 1975 Review*, 157–60.

94. The 1972 DAC report, *Development Cooperation*, discusses the critical role of agriculture and rural development at length. OECD, *Development Cooperation: Efforts and Policies of the Members of the Development Assistance Committee, 1972 Review* (Paris: OECD, 1972), 107–12, 141–50.

95. OECD, *Development Assistance: Efforts and Policies of the Members of the Development Assistance Committee, 1968 Review* (Paris: OECD, 1968), 270; OECD, *Development Cooperation: Efforts and Policies of the Members of the Development Assistance Committee, 1973 Review* (Paris: OECD, 1973), 195.

Table 4. Bank/IDA lending for directly poverty-oriented sectors as a percentage of total Bank/IDA lending (three-year averages)

Poverty-oriented Sector	Fiscal years			
	1968–1970	1971–1973	1976–1978	1979–1981
Rural development	3.2	7.6	16.5	15.3
Education (primary and nonformal)	0.2	0.8	1.4	1.6
Population, health, nutrition	—	0.7	0.6	0.3
Small-scale industry	—	0.2	1.7	1.7
Urbanization	—	1.3	2.6	3.4
Water supply/sewage	1.6	4.7	4.6	6.7
TOTAL	5.0	15.3	27.4	29.5

SOURCE: World Bank, *Focus on Poverty: A Report of a Task Force of the World Bank* (photocopy, 1982), 24.

Table 5. DAC official development assistance to the agricultural sector as a percentage of total DAC ODA

	1973	1974 (millions $U.S.)	1975
Total DAC ODA	9351	11317	13585
Agricultural assistance (broad definition)[a]	881	1767	1224
Agricultural assistance (narrow definition)[a]	802	1218	—[b]
Agriculture as percentage total (broad definition)[a]	9.4%	15.6%	9.0%
Agriculture as percentage total (narrow definition)[a]	8.6%	10.8%	—[b]

SOURCE: OECD, *Development Cooperation: 1976* (Paris: OECD, 1976), 82, 135.

[a] The *narrow* definition of agriculture includes "activities directly contributing to the development of agricultural production, such as crop development, animal husbandry, fisheries and forestry, land development and reclamation, irrigation, supply of modern means of agricultural production (especially fertilizers), agricultural services and storage facilities. The *broad* definition includes in addition agro-industries, manufacturing of modern means of production (in particular construction of fertilizer plants), rural infrastructure (when it is clearly stated that rural roads are involved) and composite projects or rural, regional, and river development." Ibid., 135, n. 3.

[b] Data under narrow definition not available for 1975.

took hold in DAC countries (well after the Bank had already shifted); the average percentage of total ODA accounted for by agricultural assistance in the entire 1979–1983 period is 17.0 percent. Thus by the beginning of the 1980s, consistently greater emphasis on agriculture seems to have been consolidated.[96]

The overall picture of bilateral assistance does not suggest leadership by the developed states on this issue. It should be noted, however, that the aggregate DAC data cited here obscure behavioral differences among donors. The social democracies of Scandinavia, in particular, have consistently had more poverty-oriented giving patterns than other OECD countries.[97] However, even if they were ahead in their poverty orientation, they do not appear to be the source of the global normative shift occurring in the early 1970s. If their poverty orientation preceded the Bank's, it seems to have had little effect on either their fellow DAC members' policies or on the policies of multilateral institutions. Certainly the Bank was not looking to or drawing from Scandinavian bilateral aid policies in any obvious way when it was rethinking its own development orientation.

The universe of development work is not limited to the World Bank and its member states. A number of other UN agencies and NGOs as well as the various regional development banks are involved in different aspects of the development effort. The International Labor Organization (ILO) was probably the most important IO contributing to the intellectual ferment which gave rise to the antipoverty focus at the Bank. The ILO's chief concern in its work was employment, however, rather than poverty per se.[98] In 1969, it launched a World Employment Program and attempted "to pioneer a new, employment-oriented approach to development"; beginning in 1970, it undertook a number of technical assistance missions to LDCs to attack unemployment and improve the conditions of workers. Later, in 1976, the ILO played an active role in the promotion of the "basic needs" approach to poverty, but by that time they were not alone in their efforts.[99]

96. OECD, *Twenty-five Years of Development Cooperation: A Review*, Paris: OECD, 1985), 214. The source does not note whether the definition of agriculture used is "broad" or "narrow."

97. Lumsdaine discusses this phenomenon in detail in *Moral Vision*, chap. 4.

98. The difference is important in that many of the world's poor are, in fact, employed, but that employment is often so badly paid that it does not provide even subsistence for workers and their families. Thus, as thinking on poverty issues in development circles continued through the 1970s, interest in employment as a means of attacking poverty—which the Bank for a time shared—gave way to other more directed programs.

99. International Labour Office, *Employment, Growth, and Basic Needs*, v–xi, 1–11.

Regional development banks were followers rather than leaders of the poverty-oriented policy shift. This is not surprising. Their small size in the general scheme of global aid flows and their regional character makes them unlikely to be catalysts of the global policy shift charted here. Indeed, the Asian Development Bank is notoriously conservative in its lending policies, and the African Development Bank has not been able to move the volume of money which would make it a major player in world development dialogues. The Inter-American Development Bank, probably the most consequential of the three regional banks, was a source of progressive social rhetoric in the sixties and early seventies under President Herrera. The Bank's lending policies, however, were driven much more by political concerns about independence from Washington and Latin American integration than by the goal of poverty alleviation. In fact, poverty alleviation is not mentioned in John White's 1972 book on the regional banks.[100] They become involved in these projects only after the World Bank had made such involvement respectable, indeed necessary.

Two other IOs that played a role in this shift were the United Nations Development Program (UNDP) and the Organization for Economic Cooperation and Development (OECD) with its Development Assistance Committee (DAC). The DAC's role has been discussed to some extent above. Unlike the Bank, the DAC's ability to translate its own changes in conviction into actual changes in development activity is limited by the compliance of its members. While the DAC did begin holding seminars and urging its members toward rural development and antipoverty policies in 1972, it is not clear that these policies changed bilateral assistance until the end of the decade. The UNDP was also active in antipoverty work in the 1970s. It issued several reports and held conferences but none before the Bank's activities were underway.[101] UNDP's influence in terms of constructing global norms was limited, however, both by the very small amount of funds at its disposal[102] and by the fact that, as a UN body operating under one state-one vote rules, it was controlled by LDCs. Within the context of the 1970s battles over the NIEO, UNDP efforts to

100. John White, *Regional Development Banks: The Asian, African, and Inter-American Development Banks* (New York: Praeger, 1972).

101. United Nations Development Program, Division of Information, *Generation: Portrait of the United Nations Development Programme, 1950–1985* (New York: United Nations, 1985), 28–30.

102. In 1969, the Bank accounted for 52.6 percent of total assistance commitments by multilateral agencies; all UN agencies combined accounted for only 10 percent. Mason and Asher, *The World Bank*, 208.

redirect North aid to the South would have been viewed with skepticism in the North.[103]

The picture that emerges is one of the World Bank as an arbiter of development norms. Before 1968, most states and even most development experts did not understand poverty alleviation to be central to the development effort. By 1975, poverty had moved to center stage. The Bank was not solely responsible for this change. It did not invent the poverty concern, nor was it the only actor promoting a poverty orientation. What the Bank did was to pick up this new approach to development and popularize it. It institutionalized the poverty focus so that it became a necessary part of development efforts by both states and international development agencies. The Bank's ability to do this stemmed from a combination of prestige and power. The intellectual prestige of the Bank's staff facilitated the persuasion of national, international, and academic development experts as to the viability and moral necessity of a poverty focus. The consequentiality of the Bank as the largest multilateral development agency gave it power to apply coercion to recalcitrant borrowers where persuasion failed. In addition, the fact that the Bank was a multilateral entity created less suspicion about its moral and humanitarian motives than might have been applied to similar actions by a single powerful state.

To say that the Bank institutionalized poverty alleviation as a central part of development does not mean that all LDC governments now act consistently for the benefit of the poor or even that the Bank consistently acts for the benefit of the poor. Like most norms, this one is violated. LDC governments may be corrupt and incompetent and therefore unable or unwilling to do anything about poverty. Such states also violated the previous norms, failing to deliver development in the form of growth. LDCs may also come under intense political pressure domestically, making redistributive policies difficult or impossible to implement. The Bank itself has been criticized for doing more harm than good with some of its poverty alleviation projects and has directed funds toward structural adjustment lending that many might argue could (and should) have gone toward poverty alleviation projects.

103. The UN Conference on Trade and Development (UNCTAD) was also caught up in NIEO battles—even more so than UNDP—and was therefore not focused on targeting aid to the poor or redefining aid norms. Furthermore, UNCTAD's mission leads it to deal much more with relations *between* states; the new policy of "targeting the poor" focused on populations *within* states.

But the existence of an antipoverty norm does mean that the collective international understanding of what development is all about has changed. Whereas before, while the existence of large impoverished populations in Asia, Africa, and Latin America was deplorable, it was, in political terms, the problem of Asians, Africans, and Latin Americans. Development was designed to create modern, industrialized, growing economies in those countries. What those states did with the fruits of growth was their own business. Making poverty alleviation a part of the international development effort changed that. It internationalized responsibility for the world's poor. In this sense it was similar to other international humanitarian moves of the postwar period that promoted human rights of various kinds. All run counter to entrenched international norms about self-determination. For this reason, they have been politically controversial but seem to be expanding rather than collapsing in the face of this opposition.

This redefinition of poverty alleviation as an international obligation may be analogous to the redefinition of poverty that occurred in the late eighteenth and nineteenth centuries at the domestic level. Before the French Revolution, the poor in Europe were largely understood through Christian religious norms—"the poor you have with you always." Attention to the poor and the giving of alms was a religious duty of individuals, and religious institutions did what they could for the poor; however, poverty was not considered a pressing problem of governments, and there was little demand or expectation that governments take responsibility for their impoverished citizenry. With the democratic revolutions of the late eighteenth and early nineteenth centuries, the rise of labor movements and of socialist parties, poverty came to be seen not simply as a problem for religious individuals and institutions, but as a shared social problem and ultimately as a political problem—one that demanded political action. The rise of the welfare state is the response to this change in social norms.[104] The institutionalization of a world antipoverty norm, conjoined with the wider human rights norms being promoted elsewhere in international politics, suggests that what occurred in the domestic political arena two hundred years ago may be expanding to the international arena. Lumsdaine's work on the foreign aid regime supports this argument. He presents evidence that the forces behind the postwar foreign aid regime are humanitarian private organizations and

---

104. Of course, these religious institutions also played a part in promoting the growth of social welfare reforms when that tide began to rise. Lumsdaine, *Moral Vision*, chap. 6.

social democratic and labor parties (the guardians of the welfare state) and then uses these facts to argue the existence of an expanded "internationalism" propelled by these groups.[105] While the power and ultimate effects of this internationalism are impossible to predict, the evidence presented here suggests that the realist reports of the death of "internationalism," may be premature.

105. Ibid.

CHAPTER FIVE

Politics in International Society

States do not always know what they want. They and the people in them develop perceptions of interest and understandings of desirable behavior from social interactions with others in the world they inhabit. States are socialized to accept certain preferences and expectations by the international society in which they and the people who compose them live.

What does it mean to say that we live in an international society? It certainly does not mean that we live in a Wilsonian or ideal world. To say that social norms are at work internationally is not to pass judgment on the ethics or morality of those norms. Some of the cases explored here, for reasons discussed in Chapter 1, emphasize what most of us would consider to be positive norms, but sociability and community can operate for good or ill. Social norms can promote slavery, racism, and ethnic cleansing as well as acts of charity and kindness.

The fact that we live in an international society means that what we want and, in some ways, who we are are shaped by the social norms, rules, understandings, and relationships we have with others. These social realities are as influential as material realities in determining behavior. Indeed, they are what endow material realities with meaning and purpose. In political terms, it is these social realities that provide us with ends to which power and wealth can be used. My concern in this book has been to demonstrate this empirically—to argue that social norms do, in fact, influence behavior and to shed some light on how they do this. One consistent finding of the cases is that norms operate in more than a regulative way. Realists and liberals of various stripes have accepted and explored norms as means of coordinating behavior among rational actors. What actors want is treated as largely unproblematic in these analyses; norms are means to Pareto improvement by regulating behavior in ways useful to actors.

The normative effects explored here go deeper. They involve reconfigurations of interests and actors in ways that cannot be accommodated within the agent-oriented perspectives that dominate political science and economics. The norms explored here are "constitutive" in the sense that they constitute, create, or revise the actors or interests which agent-oriented approaches take as given.[1] The Geneva Conventions did not provide strategic advantages to states or help them win wars. States adopted them, not as means to ends, but as ends in themselves—as affirmations of value about the kind of world people wanted and the kind of behavior that was acceptable. The incorporation of poverty alleviation goals in the development enterprise similarly did not promise to further any of the interests usually attributed to states by realist or neoliberal theories. Neither donor nor LDC states adopted these policies thinking they would become richer or more militarily secure. They adopted the policies as an expression of what they valued, of what they believed to be good and appropriate. The adoption of science bureaucracies as part of the modern state was also normative, albeit not in an ethical or moral sense. It involved a redefinition of state responsibility in a way that was unrelated to the functional needs of most states but in a way that was very much related to the normative identity of the state as an engine of progress and modernity—an identity that was particularly powerful among LDCs, where functional need for a science bureaucracy was smallest.[2]

1. For a more extensive discussion of regulative versus constitutive norms and the implications of this difference, see Alexander Wendt, *Social Theory of International Politics* (Cambridge: Cambridge University Press, forthcoming).

2. I do not mean to imply here that states do not use norms instrumentally, as means to ends. Once norms are in place, conforming to them and affirming them may bring all kinds of material benefits. The Japanese, for example, applied the Geneva Conventions unilaterally in their turn-of-the-century war against China as a way of demonstrating to European powers that they were "civilized" and so deserved to be treated as a civilized Great Power in international diplomacy, with all the benefits and privileges that status entails. But instrumental manipulation of norms in this way depends upon the norms' prior constitutive effects. States (or other actors) can be manipulated through norms only because they have internalized those norms—the norms have become part of the identity or interests of the actor. The Japanese manipulation was possible only because these norms about civilized behavior were fundamental and constitutive of European state identity and perceptions of interest. My concern in this book is with this prior issue of how certain norms come to have constitutive effects, not with subsequent manipulation of those norms.

International society and social norms thus shape or constitute the basic features of politics that most IR theory takes as given—what states want and even who or what states are. A constructivist approach can help us investigate these features of politics; other approaches cannot. It does not and it need not do this by invoking some kind of interpretivist anarchy. As the cases here show, one important characteristic of social norms is that they create patterns of behavior—patterns of the type that social science seeks to explain. A constructivist claim is that these patterns may be the result of social realities—norms and understandings—as well as the material realities emphasized by the dominant paradigms.

If we live in an international society, what kind of a society is it? What exactly are the social norms that structure and guide contemporary politics? As I noted in Chapter 1, little theorizing has been done about this. Constructivism itself only claims that social facts influence behavior; it makes no substantive claims about what those facts are any more than rational choice makes claims about the content of interests. Scholars in the American political science community whose work I would label constructivist have taken one of two directions, neither of which fills this void. Some, like Wendt and Kratochwil, have concentrated on elaborating more abstract social theory, largely setting empirical research into the content of social structure to one side. Others doing empirical work have made very narrow theoretical claims that norms matter in this or that issue area. There is no argument that norms in the various issue areas might be patterned or related to one another in a coherent way.

The cases presented here follow this latter form. They were selected to show the power of norms across a spectrum of issues in international politics. They were not selected because the norms investigated lie at critical junctures in any argument about an overarching international society. I selected cases in this way because, at present, skepticism about the causal and constitutive force of norms and our ability to investigate them empirically is widespread. Demonstrating the utility of a constructivist approach vis-à-vis dominant, interest-based paradigms is the first step in establishing a constructivist research program. The second step will be to elaborate that set of normative arguments in ways that provide more, and more easily testable, hypotheses and research questions for the future. Simply claiming that "norms matter" is not enough for constructivists. They must provide substantive arguments about which norms matter as well as how, where, and why they matter.

In this conclusion, I move in this direction by sketching a substantive argument about the normative anatomy of international society. I draw on arguments outside American political science but also on arguments in political philosophy that we know well but have not previously used. English School arguments about the expansion of the West and sociology's institutionalist arguments about Western rationalism, while different in important ways (discussed in Chapter 1), suggest similar notions about the social values that shape contemporary international life. The picture they offer is incomplete, however, notably because it pays insufficient attention to norms regarding human equality. Furthermore, these arguments overlook tensions and contradictions among social values and do not attend to the implications of those tense relationships. The result is some sharp divergences between the research agenda of sociologists in the institutionalist school and the agenda I am recommending for constructivists in political science.

My sketch of the norms underlying international society contains little that is new. Readers will recognize elements of Weber, Tocqueville, Locke, Durkheim, Marx, and others. My purpose in presenting the sketch is, first and foremost, to prompt constructivists to think seriously about the substantive content of the normative structure that we claim is so important. Others may offer corrections or alternatives to my sketch. I hope so. Without some coherent set of claims about which norms matter, constructivists will not make much headway in the discipline. With such a set of claims in hand, however, constructivism promises important insights in a world where interests are particularly fluid and interest-based paradigms are often not helpful.

A constructivist research program engages debates both inside and outside political science in new and interesting ways. It speaks to international legal scholarship and sociology, two disciplines from which political science has been largely isolated in recent years. It also speaks to issues of political philosophy and, closer to home, the attempts being made in international relations to revive a liberal paradigm. Later sections of this chapter will point out some of these connections.

The Nature of International Society

International social life at the close of the twentieth century is organized around three foundational normative elements: bureaucracies, markets, and human equality. Over the past century and, more profoundly, over the past several centuries, consensus on the goodness and appropriateness of these organizing principles of political and social life has grown and transformed international politics in the process. Bureaucracy has probably been the least contested and may be the most ubiquitous of the three. Bureaucracies, in the sense that Weber described them, are overwhelmingly understood to be *the* appropriate way to exercise authority and control in contemporary life.[3] This is true in the political realm, where power and authority are heavily bureaucratized in the state. It is true at the international level, in all types of international organizations. It is true at the sub-state and local level, and throughout most other, less overtly political, realms of social life. The garden club, the Rotary Club, and philanthropic groups all are organized in a bureaucratic fashion with presidents and secretaries and committees. Vesting authority in abstract and generalized rules which people carry out, not by virtue of any personal attributes they may have, such as lineage or charisma, but because they fill a role or position defined by rules is a distinctive hallmark of modern society, both international and otherwise.

Markets, as the legitimate way of organizing economic life, have similarly expanded to displace other, more traditional and personalistic forms of economic organization. In fact, the only serious challenger to market principles has been bureaucratic principles of economic organization such as those found in socialist economies. Bureaucracies and markets seem to be the only options for economic organization and, as of this writing, markets are clearly in the ascendence. Arguments about the expansionist character of capitalism need no rehearsal here. What is important for my purposes is the degree to which markets are viewed as legitimate, even necessary parts of economic life—so much so that many of us cannot conceive of economic life organized otherwise. Indeed, entire academic disciplines come to view *homo economicus* as some natural or inherent component of human beings. Research in anthropology, sociology, history, and area studies, of course, makes such notions untenable. Far from being natural and ubiquitous, markets are distinctly modern and Western and depend on modern, Western cultural norms for their viability. But markets have come to possess a taken-for-granted quality in modern life associated with deep-seated legitimacy. We tend to forget that markets actually require extensive normative and social support, and so we may be surprised when people have to be "taught" to be en-

3. Max Weber, *The Theory of Social and Economic Organization*, trans. A. M. Henderson and Talcott Parsons (1977; New York: Free Press, 1964), 329–42. Certainly, bureaucracy has displaced traditional, hereditary forms of authority, and charismatic authority, where it exists, is distrusted and tends, ultimately, to become bureaucratized.

trepreneurs, to set up markets, and to forego personalistic or clientelistic forms of exchange.[4]

Human equality has been, perhaps, the most overtly contested of the three norms, but it has won most of these contests, and its onward march has been made more visible because of them.[5] Debates about "who is human" and "equal with regard to what" have been and undoubtedly will continue to be centerpieces of modern politics, but the norm of human equality rarely comes under overt attack. Over the past several centuries, there has been a steady expansion of both the concept of who is human and the bases on which equality must be measured. Human equality used to mean equality of white males. Over time that meaning has expanded. Equality once meant equality of political participation only, and even then only among those of certain elevated economic means. Over time, equality has come to be measured not just in terms of political participation but also political and economic outcome.

In some ways, these three normative elements reinforce and support each other. Generalized rules and impersonal economic transactions have a certain egalitarian character in that they discriminate only with reference to characteristics related to bureaucratic aims or economic assets. The liberal democratic state is built upon a putative congruence of these norms. Its bureaucratic rules are constructed in such a way that, in conjunction with a market economy, these states can claim "equality of opportunity" as their basis of legitimacy. There are, however, tensions among these three elements as well—tensions which make stable equilibria in the search for ideal political and economic forms unlikely. Perhaps the dominant normative tension among the three is between equality and the norms of Western rationality that underpin both bureaucracies and markets. Both markets and bureaucracies are "rational" in the sense that they are impersonal, operate according to generalized rules, and are justified by claims of efficiency.[6] Ra-

4. Marc Granovetter, "Economic Action and Social Structure: The Problem of Embeddedness" *American Journal of Sociology* 91 (1985): 481–510. Joyce Oldham Appleby discusses the social construction of markets in Britain in *Economic Thought and Ideology in Seventeenth-Century England* (Princeton: Princeton University Press, 1978). For a more general "denaturalizing" treatment of economics as a discipline, see Donald N. McCloskey, *The Rhetoric of Economics* (Madison: University of Wisconsin Press, 1985).

5. Alexis de Tocqueville is, of course, the great exponent of the power and social effects of human equality. See *Democracy in America*, ed. J. P. Mayer, trans. George Lawrence (New York: Doubleday, 1969).

6. There are and have been other non-rational, normative principles on which to justify economic and social life—systems based on divine ordination, patrimonial rights, equality of outcome—which would be, and must be, personalistic and particularistic in the way they operate.

tional rules need not and perhaps usually do not have equal results. The application of general rules to groups of dissimilar human beings (no two people being alike) often creates unequal outcomes. The tendency of markets to produce unequal outcomes, even under conditions of equal access, is well known. The result is continued calls for bureaucratic intervention against markets in the service of equality. Bureaucratic states mandate social safety nets, affirmative action programs, and other redresses to perceived inequalities created by the marketplace.

The World Bank case discussed in Chapter 4 reflects this normative conflict at the international level. In that case, an international bureaucracy asserted the rights of all people to the satisfaction of "basic human needs" and intervened in international and national markets as well as state bureaucracies to advance that normative claim. The science policy case can also be understood as international bureaucratic intervention to mitigate perceived market failures. In that case, the market was a "market of ideas." Because developing states had become increasingly suspicious about the unequal distributions created by international markets and dissatisfied with the slow "trickle-down" of technological know-how from the North, the creation of science bureaucracies was in part an attempt to remedy perceived failures in the international market of scientific ideas through state intervention and to create a more equal distribution of scientific knowledge.

Bureaucracy does not always serve equality. It, too, can offend. Bureaucratic rules, being general and impersonal, may discriminate generally and impersonally against whole classes of people. "Rights" claims, usually rooted in the equality norm, have been used by a variety of groups to attack such rule categories. The result is extensive debates over the meaning of equality—who is equal and equal with regard to what. The abolition of slavery was one obvious assertion of equality rights against the bureaucratic allocation of property rights, but similar debates continue over the differential treatment of women, children, the elderly, and the disabled, to name a few. At the international level, claims about "human rights" have become increasingly consequential and have given rise to attacks on many state bureaucracies. Often it is IOs—international bureaucracies—that intervene against states in the name of human rights. Red Cross actions, described in Chapter 3, can be understood as one early instance of this. The fundamental humanitarian claim of the ICRC is that all noncombatants are equally deserving of humanitarian treatment, even enemies.

In addition to being in tension with equality claims, markets and bureaucracies stand in tension with one another. Markets need some amount of bureaucratic involvement simply to function. The large literature on market failures and the need for bureaucracies (particularly the state) to provide certain collective goods that make contracting and other essential market functions possible is well known. However, bureaucracies tend to undermine the efficiency of markets that is their claim to legitimacy and social value. Similarly, bureaucracies alone appear to be incapable of ordering modern economies in ways that satisfy demands for progress and material accumulation by citizens. The failed Soviet experiment is ample testimony to this. Without market mechanisms bureaucracies cannot produce viable economies. Questions about how much and what type of state intervention in markets is desirable or what degree of market corrective to state authoritative allocation is necessary are not easily resolved.

THE POLITICS OF INTERNATIONAL NORMS

Tensions and contradictions among normative principles in international life mean that there is no set of ideal political and economic arrangements toward which we are all converging. There is no stable equilibrium, no end of history. All good things do not and probably cannot go together. Instead, social institutions are continually being contested, albeit to varying degrees at different times. Unresolved normative tensions in a set of social compromises at one time may be the mobilizing force for attacks on that set of social arrangements later, as people articulate normative claims that earlier were pushed aside.[7]

These contestation processes are political. In fact, normative contestation is in large part what politics is all about: competing values and understandings of what is good, desirable, and appropriate in our collective, communal life. Debates about civil rights, affirmative action, social safety nets, regulation and deregulation, and the appropriate degree of government intrusion into the lives of citizens are all debates precisely because there is no clear stable normative solution. Furthermore,

7. The treatment of slavery in the United States is an example of an issue for which there was no stable solution, and normative claims denied came back to force change. Constitutional framers legitimated their entire revolution and political project on claims of human equality yet made compromises with market forces that allowed slavery to continue. Those claims came back during the Civil War and were used to define the purpose of the war for the North. In fact, much of the Civil War can be viewed as a contest over the meaning of equality: was it equality for states (states' rights?), equality for whites, or equality for all?

they are all debates involving conflict among the basic normative "goods" identified earlier. Debates about civil rights, affirmative action, and to some extent social safety nets are debates about the nature of equality—who gets to be equal and how equality is measured. Since the solutions all involve bureaucratic intervention, these debates are also about the relationship of bureaucracies and the state to equality. Debates about social safety nets raise specific issues about the relationship of bureaucracies and markets and the degree to which the latter may be compromised by the former in the service of equality. Debates over regulation and government intrusion are both about the degree to which bureaucracy can compromise markets *or* equality and the individual liberties that derive from equality.

Assuming a normative structure that contains competing and contradictory elements forces constructivists to attend to both politics and process. Norms of international society may create similar structures and push both people and states toward similar behavior, but the body of international norms is not completely congruent. Certainly, it is not congruent enough to produce homogeneity or equifinality. Tensions and contradictions among the norms leave room for different solutions and different arrangements, each of which makes legitimacy claims based on the same norms. The compromises arrived at may be contingent on local circumstances and personalities and are likely to reflect the local norms and customs with which international norms have had to compromise. International norms may have persuaded all states that they needed science bureaucracies, but the bureaucracies in Germany, Romania, and Botswana look quite different from one another. More generically, international norms may dictate that the state is *the* appropriate form of political organization, yet there is room for wide variety in the form of governing arrangements within those acceptable international normative parameters. The particular form of any state is a result of both international and local factors.

These local variations are not simply oddities of interest only to area specialists. Some contingent, local results may become internationalized and institutionalized as part of the global normative structure in important ways, thus influencing the content of international normative structure at a later time. Watershed events such as the French and Russian revolutions may have occurred for local and contingent reasons, but the normative claims they made—the interpretations they articulated and defended of equality and, in the Russian case, of the desirable relationships between bureaucracy and markets—became internationalized and influenced global normative understandings of equality, markets, and state bureaucracies in lasting ways.

It is this interaction between international structures and local agents of change that interests constructivists. It is not enough for constructivists to look only at international normative structures and their effects. They must also focus on the origins and dynamics of these norms, a focus which inevitably takes them into a world of agents. In these case studies, I have demonstrated the widespread effects of the norms in question and presented analyses of the origins and dynamics of these norms that highlight political contestation and agency. The agents investigated here were transnational-level actors, both IOs and the individuals in them. One could examine other agent relationships with these norms, focusing most obviously on the ways in which these norms worked their effects inside the many states of the system and, perhaps, the ways in which the norms were eventually affected by those individual state experiences. I chose not to do this both because of the theoretical reasons for my interest in IOs, described in Chapter 1, and for the practical reason that a study of this global breadth cannot also provide in-depth analysis of the politics within individual states. Nonetheless, I would applaud efforts of others in this direction.[8]

This constructivist concern with agency and politics sets it apart from the ongoing research among institutionalists in sociology. The concern of sociologists has been to demonstrate normative effects by searching for patterns of similarity across a range of dissimilar actors. Functional or interest-maximizing explanations would expect dissimilar behavior from actors with dissimilar utility functions. Norms, however, may make similar claims on dissimilar actors and so would account for these patterns. The result has been that the institutionalists in sociology have compiled an impressive collection of examples of the power of international norms on state and sub-state behavior in areas as diverse as the writing of national constitutions, the composition of school curricula, national welfare policies, definitions of citizenship, and weapons acquisition policies.[9] As dis-

8. I have tried to note individual state experiences where they appear relevant to the international normative structure. For example, I discuss the origins of science policy bureaucracies in several states in Chapter 2, individual state reactions to the Geneva conventions proposals in Chapter 3, and unusual aid policies in the Scandinavian states in Chapter 4.

9. George M. Thomas, John W. Meyer, Francisco O. Ramirez, and John Boli, eds., *Institutional Structure: Constituting State, Society, and the Individual* (Newbury Park, Calif.: Sage Publications, 1987); Albert Bergesen, ed., *Studies of the Modern World-System* (New York: Academic Press, 1980); David Strang and Patricia Mei Yin Chang, "The International Labor Organization and the Welfare State: Institutional Effects on National Welfare Spending,

cussed in Chapter 1, these institutionalists have offered a synthetic understanding of the origins and content of the norms they document, one that emphasizes rationality and Western notions of modernity and progress.

The sociologists' work is well worth the attention of political scientists, both for the methods employed and for the coherence of their argument. They offer a macro-level theoretical approach that can explain much that our dominant paradigms cannot, and they use rigorous quantitative methods that would bring a smile to the most hardened positivist. What is missing is attention to politics and process. Sociologists offer little discussion of or research on where these norms come from, the mechanisms by which they influence states, and how they change over time. However, I see nothing to prevent such investigation. Case studies to complement large-N analyses could easily be done to fill this gap and would provide yet more bases for conversation between our disciplines.

The lack of attention to politics may result from a more fundamental disagreement between the sociologists and the approach I outline here. My international society is one in which basic norms are not in complete congruence. At times, they may make countervailing claims on people or mobilize groups with opposing claims, both of which are grounded in basic, legitimate norms of society. The institutionalists' view does not emphasize and may not even acknowledge that such conflicts exist. The suggestion implicit in their research program is that the world is in the grips of a global homogenization process. Weberian rationality is marching relentlessly across the earth, leaving in its wake a marketized, bureaucratized world of increasingly similar forms. If the norms of what they call the "world polity" (or what I would call international society) are at odds in fundamental ways, these conflicts have not been researched or emphasized. They should be.

The issue is whether isomorphism implies equifinality—whether similar, norm-conforming behavior across the international system will have

1960–1980," *International Organization* 47 (1993): 235–62; John Meyer, Francisco Ramirez, Richard Rubinson, and John Boli-Bennett, "The World Educational Revolutions, 1950–1970," *Sociology of Education* 50 (1977): 242–58; Yasemin Soysal, *The Limits of Citizenship: Migrants and Postnational Membership in Europe* (Chicago: University of Chicago Press, 1995); Dana P. Eyre and Mark C. Suchman, "Status, Norms, and the Proliferation of Conventional Weapons: An Instiutional Theory Approach," in Peter Katzenstein, ed., *The Culture of National Security: Norms and Identity in World Politics* (New York: Columbia University Press, 1996). For a review of this work and its implications for political science see Martha Finnemore, "Norms, Culture, and World Politics: Insights from Sociology's Institutionalism," *International Organization*, 50 (spring 1996): 325–47.

equal results and create a homogeneous system. I have suggested that the constructivists' answer to this is a strong *no*. Conflicts among norms have no unique solutions. Different and shifting solutions will be tried in different places, and local context becomes important in identifying the particular solutions that will be tried in each place. Human equality may gain global recognition as a necessary good, but notions about human equality may differ in Islamic states, socialist states, and West European states. Ideas about the appropriate place of market forces may differ even between European and North American states. The triumph of core international norms may create gross secular changes in international politics by delegitimating and effectively eliminating some forms of behavior (as, for example, the human equality norm has eliminated slavery), but it still leaves substantial room for interpretation and contestation, particularly in light of other strong norms in international life. It is not clear how the institutionalists in sociology would respond to the question of whether isomorphism implies equifinality, but their research suggests a much stronger expectation of ultimate similarity of outcome, of growing uniformity in the world, than a constructivist would have. This expectation flows logically from the normative specification with which they begin. To the extent that world norms are congruent rather than conflicting, pressures for equifinality grow.

CONSTRUCTIVISM AND INTERNATIONAL LAW

The notion that norms, understandings, and discourse shape state behavior is hardly news to many outside political science. International legal scholars have always known this: norms are their bread and butter. At the international level norms *are* the law. Customary international law exists only when states share an understanding that compliance with some rule of behavior is necessary and appropriate. Customary international law exists only where there is a norm. A constructivist approach in political science opens up possibilities for conversation with international legal scholars that were foreclosed under realist domination of our discipline. Realism has not been interested in international law. In fact, realism doubts not only the relevance but even the existence of such law. From a realist perspective, "law," or the appearance of it, is only an epiphenomenon of power politics. What order and rules exist in international politics survive because they are in the interest of strong states and are established and enforced by the strong. Concern with legal maxims and rationalizations only obscures the fundamental dynamics of state behavior.[10]

Constructivists, by contrast, take the causal force of norms and understandings seriously and undertake analyses of their nature and effects that speak directly to the interests of legal scholars. International legal scholarship should be interesting to constructivists in at least two ways. First, the nature of the analytical enterprise is similar. When lawyers argue and courts or tribunals decide matters of customary international law, they are looking for *opinio juris*—evidence that states share a belief that some principle is law. The methods for doing so look much like the methods used by constructivist scholars in political science to establish the existence of a norm. They look at behavior and ask whether states act as if there is, in fact, such a norm. Additionally, they look at discourse and ask if states justify actions by identifying and emphasizing the importance of the norm or principle. When adjudicating norm violations, they ask whether the conflict is at the level of norm or fact, that is, whether violators are challenging the norm or challenging interpretations of fact (such as whether particular events occurred and if they occurred, whether they are prohibited under the norm). As investigatory efforts the two are similar.

Second, international legal scholarship is an interesting object of study for constructivists in that part of its mission is to make new norms. One of the functions of legal scholarship is to articulate and codify norms and rules for states. The status of scholarly writings as authoritative sources to be used in the efforts of courts to discern the law has been accepted for centuries. It is made explicit in the founding statute of the International Court of Justice, which lists the sources of international law in Article 38. Writings from "publicists" or noted legal scholars can be and are offered as evidence of the existence of a norm of customary international law. Their interpretations of state behavior and whether it establishes the existence of a norm have legal standing.

There are reasons to think that legal scholars' prescriptions for state behavior have some influence. Scholarly writings often inform the text of treaties and other agreements among states, and international lawyers are

10. Obviously, the body of international law is much larger than customary international law; nonetheless, customary law is the part of that larger corpus that throws the constructivist and realist relationships to law into starkest relief. For a short history of the relationship between international law and international relations, see Anne-Marie Slaughter Burley, "International Law and International Relations Theory: A Dual Agenda," *American Journal of International Law* 87 (1993): 205–39.

almost always instrumental in writing these documents. Similarly, it is the arguments of lawyers and international jurists about the ways in which these agreements should be interpreted that shape outcomes in conflicts over international legal norms. The most serious and fundamental normative conflicts will only be settled politically, but much of the lower-level, day-to-day international normative conflict is fought out and settled by lawyers in national and international courts and tribunals.[11] In these legal forums the decision rule is normative consistency as determined through logical argumentation. Normative claims become powerful and prevail by being persuasive; being persuasive means grounding claims in existing norms in ways that emphasize normative congruence and coherence.[12] Persuasiveness and logical coherence of normative claims are important politically, but are essential and must be explicit in law.[13]

Conventional IR theories cannot talk about persuasion. The consequentialist, utility-maximizing foundations of neorealism and neoliberalism leave no room for it. New information may influence strategic choice, but the crafting of argument and the art of persuasion—of changing what people value or think is right and good—have no place in these accounts of state behavior. Yet, as lawyers and politicians know, rhetorical processes are vital to the success of a case or a policy. If rational choice theorists were right, neither lawyers nor politicians would spend so much time talking. However, much of politics is talk—attempts to persuade or justify. The fact that policymakers spend so much time on rhetoric and on selling policies to publics, allies, and enemies is something that we should take seriously. It does not make much sense in a standard neorealist or neoliberal framework of strategic interaction in which actors know what they want. Persuasion then is a waste of time. It makes a great deal of sense,

11. Virtually all states now recognize international law as part of their body of domestic law, though interpretations of the relationship between the two vary. In the United States, the seminal statement of this came in the *Paquete Habana* case. Elsewhere, national constitutions often explicitly make this incorporation.

12. For an excellent exposition of this, see Thomas M. Franck, *The Power of Legitimacy among Nations* (New York: Oxford University Press, 1990), especially chaps. 9 and 10. Normative and legal congruence are not the only standards by which courts may decide. The International Court of Justice is explicitly empowered to make judgements on the basis of simple "equity and justice" when it deems necessary. See Statute of the International Court of Justice, Article 38, Section 2. The notion that there is such a standard at all implies some kind of overarching normative framework for international dealings beyond what is spelled out in international law—an implication that might interest constructivists.

13. The emphasis on logic and deductive reasoning in ascertaining persuasiveness is very Western and fits well with the claims made by both English School and sociological institutionalist scholars about the triumph of Western norms and Western rationality in contemporary international society.

however, from a constructivist perspective. It indicates the degree to which people's preferences are malleable and reveals the opportunities for agents to manipulate social rules or be driven by them. Much normative conflict and change occurs in a legal framework. Constructivists need to understand the rules by which lawyers persuade and judges or arbiters adjudicate among norms—what makes a normative claim persuasive and compelling—if they are to understand mutual constitution processes of agents and structures at the international level.

Law thus offers constructivists interesting avenues for research, but the relationship is reciprocal. Constructivism should be interesting for legal scholars because it engages the central social scientific debates with realism that have forced international law to defend its relevance, even its existence, for so many years.[14] Drawing on social psychological and organization theory literatures, constructivism provides arguments about why, at the most basic level, behavior may be rule-driven. It seeks to provide a social theoretical foundation for law's claim that its norms and rules shape behavior in ways that are not simply epiphenomenal of interests. Linking law with behavior even in the absence of enforcement has been the critical missing component of law's response to realism.

Constructivism, like realism or any of the other approaches in social science, is concerned with explaining why states behave as they do. It is explanatory and descriptive. Law, by contrast, is largely *prescriptive*, concerned with codifying and reconciling rules of behavior for states. Questions about why these rules and not others exist or why states comply or do not comply with them are peripheral to the realm of law.[15] They are, however, central to constructivists, who are fundamentally concerned with questions about why some rules or norms exist and not others and why states comply with those rules, as the empirical cases in this book show.

At the heart of the realist challenge is the fact that international law has no social theoretical microfoundations. It is easy to prescribe: anyone can dream up desirable rules and happy futures. The hard job is to artic-

14. See Burley, "International Law and International Relations Theory," 205–9.
15. Legal scholars have delved into these issues on occasion, producing important insights from their legal perspective. Franck's *The Power of Legitimacy among Nations* and Louis Henkin's *How Nations Behave: Law and Foreign Policy* (New York: Praeger, 1968) are excellent examples. But inquiries of this kind are not the core of day-to-day international legal activity. The fact that Abram and Antonia Chayes's recent article "On Compliance" appeared in the political science journal *International Organization* 47 (1993): 175–205 rather than the *American Journal of International Law* is suggestive of the way in which these behavioral issues are not always central to the mainstream of legal inquiry.

ulate a set of desirable rules that have some chance of being followed, given what we know about behavior. If prescription is not based on some fairly explicit understandings about behavior, about why international politics works as it does, law's prescriptions will be dismissed as the kind of "idealism" that was discredited in political science in the 1930s.[16] By explaining why and how behavior may be norm-governed, constructivism deals precisely with issues that are microfoundational for international law and so can help law respond to the realists.

CONSTRUCTIVISM AND LIBERALISM

Constructivists are not the only group to become interested in the question of how states know what they want. Liberals have regrouped in recent years and redefined a framework for investigating state behavior that differs from their "neo" counterparts—a framework that problematizes state preference formation. It is an important argument with a long pedigree in political science, and its relationship to constructivism needs to be clarified.[17] Whereas neoliberal institutionalists have chosen to engage neorealists by black-boxing the state and treating states and their interests as given, exponents of liberalism as a mode of analysis have chosen to stay closer to the philosophical roots of liberal thought. For them, states are rooted in and derive from civil society. All states are constituted by civil society, and their policies reflect the interests of one or more groups in domestic society. State preferences are thus the preferences of dominant domestic groups. Foreign policy, therefore, cannot be derived simply or automatically from external positional calculations about the balance of power in the system. Even external threats and con-

16. E. H. Carr, *The Twenty Years' Crisis, 1919–1939: An Introduction to the Study of International Relations* (New York: Harper & Row, 1964).

17. Moravcsik's formulation of this version of liberalism is probably the most ambitious and recent. See Andrew Moravcsik, "Liberalism and International Relations Theory," Center for International Affairs, Harvard University, Working Paper 92–6, revised April 1993. For an application of the argument, see Moravcsik, "Preferences and Power in the European Community: A Liberal Intergovernmentalist Approach," *Journal of Common Market Studies* 31 (1993): 473–524. Particularly influential among the earlier, pre-"neo" liberals were Robert O. Keohane and Joseph S. Nye, *Power and Interdependence: World Politics in Transition* (Boston: Little, Brown, 1977). A rather different framework that contains the essential elements of liberal analysis appears in James N. Rosenau, *Turbulence in World Politics* (Princeton: Princeton University Press, 1990). For applications of liberal analysis to international law, see Anne-Marie (Slaughter) Burley, "Liberal States: A Zone of Law" (Paper delivered at the Annual Meeting of the American Political Science Association, Chicago, September 1992), and "International Relations Theory and International Law."

straints are perceived by and filtered through domestic political processes and structures that shape policy outputs in important ways.[18]

This kind of liberalism shares three important characteristics with the constructivist argument I outline here: it is concerned with state preferences and does not assume them; it sees states as embedded in a larger social context; and it recognizes a wide variety of non-state actors as consequential in world politics. The first two propositions are central to any constructivist analysis and have been treated extensively in Chapter 1. The third claim is more controversial. In agreeing with liberals on this third claim, I depart from more statist constructivists, such as Alexander Wendt, who make state-centrism a core assumption of their argument. While there are certain practical and tactical reasons to focus on states— they are big and powerful, and such a focus allows one to engage neorealism and neoliberalism on their own turf—I see no theoretical reasons to make this commitment. There is nothing about the logic of constructivism that would lead one to privilege states and, as the studies in this book show, constructivist analysis often underscores the importance of non-state agents and non-state social structures in global social construction processes.[19]

The social world of states is varied. I have focused on the role IOs play in shaping state interests, but social norms and shared values influence perceptions of interests and patterns of behavior across the spectrum of possible actors and at all levels of international politics. They can shape expectations in bilateral state relationships without IOs to mediate, creating both friends—e.g., the "special relationship" between the United Kingdom and the United States that persisted long past Britain's power capabilities—and enemies—e.g., the shift from alliance to Cold War in the

18. Both Moravcsik and Slaughter (Burley) have argued that state preferences are also embedded in transnational society—a claim that speaks directly to the research design of this book. In their studies of the European Union, both have suggested how, empirically, this might occur, but it is not clear how their claim squares with Moravcsik's social scientific analytical framework. His three core assumptions all situate states in *domestic* society and make them representative of that society. If transnational social preferences reach state policy only through their adoption and assertion by domestic actors, then transnational society's influence is only indirect. States are "embedded" in transnational society only to the extent that domestic society is "embedded" in transnational society. Direct influence of transnational actors on state decisionmakers, of the sort documented in this book and of the sort that are quite common in the EU, would be hard to explain. But if states are embedded directly in a transnational society, then Moravcsik's assumptions and ontology need to be clarified.

19. Alexander Wendt, "Collective Identity Formation and the International State," *American Political Science Review* 88 (1994): 384–96, and *Social Theory of International Politics*, chap. 1.

U.S.-Soviet relationship. At a systemic level, norms among states can also create shared expectations for multilateralism.[20] Localized social understandings among domestic groups may also influence state policy, giving states certain identities and predictable characteristics in international interactions. Long-held Swiss consensus about neutrality would be one example. Scandanavian internationalism and humanitarianism, stemming from domestic norms, would be another.[21] A third would be the way that shared understandings within Japan about the relationship between economic and social institutions support distinctive and controversial trade policies by that state. Finally, social norms and the interactions that support them can be transnational, linking domestic publics, IOs, and states, as they frequently are linked in human rights and environmental politics.[22]

States are embedded in an international social fabric that extends from the local to the transnational. Local events experienced by particular individuals can have transnational effects, as the case of Henry Dunant and the Red Cross illustrates. Transnational politics and the structure of system-level actors can have very localized effects, as demonstrated by the World Bank's targeting of small farmers in rural development projects. The international society suggested by these cases is not a society of states of the kind posited by the English school or by Wendt. It is a society that looks much more like the world of complex interdependence or turbulence described by liberals in the variety of actors it recognizes and in the blurring of old-fashioned "levels of analysis" created by the transnational linkages it investigates.[23]

Despite these shared concerns, the argument offered here differs from liberalism as a mode of social science analysis in at least two ways. First, the great variety of actors recognized within a liberal analysis are

20. John G. Ruggie, ed., *Multilateralism Matters: The Theory and Praxis of an Institutional Form* (New York: Columbia University Press, 1993).

21. David Halloran Lumsdaine, *Moral Vision in International Politics: The Foreign Aid Regime, 1949–1989* (Princeton: Princeton University Press, 1993).

22. Kathryn Sikkink, "Human Rights, Principled Issue-Networks and Sovereignty in Latin America," *International Organization* 47 (1993): 411–41; Thomas Risse-Kappen, ed., *Bringing Transnational Relations Back In: Non-State Actors, Domestic Structures and International Institutions* (Cambridge: Cambridge University Press, 1995).

23. The terms "complex interdependence" and "turbulence" are central in Keohane and Nye, *Power and Interdependence*, and Rosenau, *Turbulence in World Politics*. Strict adherence to levels of analysis has been advocated most influentially in Kenneth Waltz, *Man, the State, and War: A Theoretical Analysis* (New York: Columbia University Press, 1959), and *Theory of International Politics* (New York: Random House, 1979), and in J. David Singer, "The Level-of-analysis Problem in International Relations," *World Politics* 14 (1961): 77–92. The notion that these levels can profitably be separated has continued to dominate thinking in the field.

not bound together in any predictable or patterned way. Liberalism sees a world full of actors pursuing lots of interests and leaves researchers little guidance about what is important or where to start their work. In a framework in which all kinds of actors matter and virtually every outcome is in somebody's interest, analysis quickly becomes intractable and outcomes are often overdetermined. By specifying a social structure with a particular normative content which all of these varied actors inhabit, the approach I outline does suggest patterns of behavior and focal points for conflict—where, for example, markets, bureaucracies, and equality conflict. The interests of actors cannot be just anything; they must be patterned and follow prevailing understandings of the culture in which actors act. I have already given some suggestions about the nature of those understandings at the broadest level. Mapping these global cultural understandings and understanding their dynamics of change provide a focus for constructivist research.

Second, and more fundamental, while the research agenda for liberals involves analyzing the formation of state preferences—a project very similar to the one I lay out here—the ways in which we go about this are very different. Specifically, liberalism does not provide a basis for treating preferences as malleable and an outgrowth of affective social interaction. Underlying preferences cannot change in liberal analysis. The system-wide preference shifts I investigate in this book—cases in which preferences about ends change as a result of interaction among states and individuals who share understandings about legitimacy and community—cannot be accommodated in a liberal framework.

Like neorealism and neoliberalism, liberalism imputes preferences; it just imputes them one or more levels down below the level of the state, to individuals and groups. When liberals investigate state preference formation, what they are really doing is investigating preference aggregation. Everybody in civil society (where analysis presumably starts) already knows what they want; the question is who will prevail in the domestic struggle to control state policy.[24] This preference aggregation process differs from the constructivist questions I pose here. It is concerned with understanding the ways in which various domestic and transnational ac-

24. Preference formation in this liberal view does not appear to be very different from the way realists were characterizing it in the 1970s, before neoliberalism hit the stage. It is essentially a pluralist view of politics. See Robert Gilpin, *U.S. Power and the Multinational Corporation: The Political Economy of Direct Investment* (New York: Basic Books, 1975), chap. 1, and Stephen D. Krasner, *Defending the National Interest: Raw Materials Investments and U.S. Foreign Policy* (Princeton: Princeton University Press, 1978), chap. 1, for realist summaries of this kind of liberalism.

tors interact and compete to pull state policy in their preferred direction. Why groups or individuals want what they want is not a subject of liberal inquiry; their wants must be assumed before analysis can proceed.

Liberal analysis of this type can tell us a great deal, for interest group competition and its associated push-pull on state policy is a ubiquitous feature of politics. Liberal analyses can become quite sophisticated, incorporating insights about principal-agent relationships, bounded rationality, transaction costs, and limited information to make sense of convoluted and counterintuitive policies that emerge from interstate bargaining. It cannot, however, address the kinds of issues I investigate and ask questions about changes in collectively shared social values or definitions of what is good and appropriate. The reason for this lies in a longstanding tension deeply rooted in liberal normative theory. The tension, in a philosophical sense, comes from liberalism's elevation of individual choice as the locus of "the good" when individuals are not and cannot be self-sufficient or self-contained, morally and ethically. Liberalism rests fundamentally on a set of normative claims about individual self-sufficiency in a moral sense. Individuals know "the good," and satisfaction of their wants *is* "the good" in the sense of being the appropriate goal of politics. Guaranteeing individual rights and liberties so that individuals can pursue happiness is the goal toward which liberal politics is directed.

In social science, liberalism's corollary to this normative individualism is methodological individualism. Such analysis can be very useful, but it is fundamentally different from the constructivist approach, for methodological individualism is an actor- or agent-oriented approach. As such, it has both the virtues and the limitations of approaches on that side of the structure-agent debate, as discussed in Chapter 1. One of the limitations is that it cannot accommodate constitutive social forces that create new interests or reshape actors. Within a liberal framework, individuals may learn new strategies in response to new information or change their course of action because of changed constraints and opportunities inside some new institutional structure in which they find themselves, but underlying preferences must remain constant. There is no room for normative sea changes that shift basic social goals and values. Methodological individualism cannot tell us very much about the socialization and persuasion processes that change what we value; it cannot address the ways in which what we want and who we are become shaped by culture and society. To the extent that we are products of the cultures and social values with which we live, methodological individualism is of little help in explaining these variations in behavior across time and space.

Liberal philosophy has understood the importance of social context for individual choice for a long time. Tocqueville, one of its best-known analysts, understood clearly the political dangers not just of inward-looking self-interest, but of individuals' claims to moral self-sufficiency. To combat the former, he applauded associations, newspapers, and the like; to combat the latter, he was convinced of the necessity of religion. Other liberal philosophers have similarly emphasized the need for different elements of affect and community to create viable and desirable polities. Smith and Hume are very concerned with "sentiment" and morality as well as reason and rights. Education in Mill and Rousseau is not just the imparting of information; it is the creation of affective bonds that change and reconstitute preferences.[25]

While the tension between community and individuals, between affect and self-interest, has enlivened and enriched liberal philosophy, it is not easily accommodated in liberal social science. The response of liberal social science has been to jettison this concern in order to retain methodological individualism, with the result that, from a constructivist perspective, the liberal "society" specified by social scientists using the term is not very social.[26] It is a collection of individuals who interact and who may choose to form institutional arrangements through which they can further their individual welfare. But the glue or "cement," to use Jon Elster's term, of this society is very thin.[27] There is no culture and little affect. Normative content, to the extent it exists, is regulative, not constitutive. People may choose to create norms that are Pareto-improving but those norms are instrumental. They may intervene between basic interests and behavior, but they are not causal. Norms do not reconfigure properties of actors: they have no prior ontological status. Investigating the most basic political questions about social purpose and political values requires a constructivist approach.

Different theoretical approaches allow us to ask different questions. The questions I investigate in this book concern the goals of interna-

25. For a related argument, see Joshua Mitchell, *Not by Reason Alone: Religion, History, and Identity in Early Modern Political Thought* (Chicago: University of Chicago Press, 1993).

26. Liberal society in philosophy can be very rich in this sense, but, as noted above, philosophy recognizes the inadequacy of the individual self-sufficiency assumption used by social science and is not hamstrung by it. Indeed, it may be precisely the tension in philosophic liberalism between individual and community—so intractable to social scientists—that accounts for its richness and resilience in philosophy.

27. As noted in Chapter 1, Elster's "cement" is also rather weak from the perspective I outline in that it, too, is neither generative nor constitutive. Jon Elster, *The Cement of Society: A Study of Social Order* (New York: Cambridge University Press, 1989).

tional political life and how those change over time. These are basic questions, yet they have been off the table for international relations scholars for most of this century. The climate of the Cold War and the economistic models of politics that flourished during it supported forms of analysis in which these questions were simply assumed away. In a dangerous world survival was the only goal, and theories composed solely of constraints were deemed sufficient to provide satisfactory explanations of behavior. Looking back, most political scientists now see choice as well as constraint. Looking forward, constraints look even less clear, and questions about what U.S. goals should be in the world are more pressing and less easily answered. I offer no policy prescriptions or predictions in this book. My more modest claim is simply that the policy goals that will emerge for the next century will be formed at least in part by the international social context in which we live. Normative valuation on multilateralism and human rights, as well as democracy and market economies, will create new political agendas for the United States. Some, such as the expanded set of humanitarian military interventions under UN auspices, would have been unthinkable during the Cold War. Others, such as the expanded power of international organizations and international legal instruments in issue areas concerning the environment and human rights, are extensions of processes that have been going on for decades.

We can understand changes in this normative fabric of international politics only if we investigate the shared understandings that underlie it. Doing so requires a fundamentally different approach from the actor-oriented, economistic approaches we have been using for 50 years. Taking a sociological turn and treating social relations as social realities that shape behavior as much as material realities allows us to do this.

Index

Cornell Studies in Political Economy

EDITED BY PETER J. KATZENSTEIN

National Diversity and Global Capitalism edited by Suzanne Berger and
  Ronald Dore
Collapse of an Industry: Nuclear Power and the Contradictions of U. S. Policy
  by John L. Campbell
The Price of Wealth: Economics and Institutions in the Middle East
  by Kiren Aziz Chaudhry
Power, Purpose, and Collective Choice: Economic Strategy in Socialist States
  edited by Ellen Comisso and Laura Tyson
The Political Economy of the New Asian Industrialism edited by Frederic C. Deyo
Dislodging Multinationals: India's Strategy in Comparative Perspective
  by Dennis J. Encarnation
Rivals beyond Trade: America versus Japan in Global Competition
  by Dennis J. Encarnation
Enterprise and the State in Korea and Taiwan by Karl J. Fields
National Interests in International Society by Martha Finnemore
Democracy and Markets: The Politics of Mixed Economies by John R. Freeman
The Misunderstood Miracle: Industrial Development and Political Change in Japan
  by David Friedman
*Patchwork Protectionism: Textile Trade Policy in the United States, Japan, and West
  Germany* by H. Richard Friman
Ideas and Foreign Policy: Beliefs, Institutions, and Political Change
  edited by Judith Goldstein and Robert O. Keohane
Ideas, Interests, and American Trade Policy by Judith Goldstein
Monetary Sovereignty: The Politics of Central Banking in Western Europe
  by John B. Goodman
Politics in Hard Times: Comparative Responses to International Economic Crises
  by Peter Gourevitch
Cooperation among Nations: Europe, America, and Non-tariff Barriers to Trade
  by Joseph M. Grieco
*Nationalism, Liberalism, and Progress, Volume 1: The Rise and Decline of
  Nationalism* by Ernst B. Haas
*Pathways from the Periphery: The Politics of Growth in the Newly Industrializing
  Countries* by Stephan Haggard
The Politics of Finance in Developing Countries edited by Stephan Haggard,
  Chung H. Lee, and Sylvia Maxfield
*Rival Capitalists: International Competitiveness in the United States, Japan, and
Western Europe* by Jeffrey A. Hart
The Philippine State and the Marcos Regime: The Politics of Export
  by Gary Hawes
Reasons of State: Oil Politics and the Capacities of American Government
  by G. John Ikenberry
The State and American Foreign Economic Policy edited by G. John Ikenberry,
  David A. Lake, and Michael Mastanduno
The Nordic States and European Unity by Christine Ingebritsen
*The Paradox of Continental Production: National Investment Policies in North
  America* by Barbara Jenkins
Pipeline Politics: The Complex Political Economy of East-West Energy Trade
  by Bruce W. Jentleson
The Government of Money: Monetarism in Germany and the United States
  by Peter A. Johnson
The Politics of International Debt edited by Miles Kahler